ABC's
OF
PEAK
PERFORMERS

ABC's
OF
PEAK
PERFORMERS

26 Simple Steps to a More
Empowered, Joyful Life

Bill Poett

SEA·HILL
PRESS

Santa Barbara

Sea Hill Press, Inc.
www.seahillpress.com
Santa Barbara, California
Book design and layout: Walter Sharp

Cover design: Lucinda Kinch

ISBN 978-0-9708050-5-8
Library of Congress Control Number: 2011926781

Printed in the United States of America

DEDICATED TO

. . . you, my reader. You have been my muse and the driving force behind this book for longer than you can imagine. Mary Louise and Harold Poett, my mom and dad, for providing me with the love, foundation, and education to become the husband, father, and coach I am today. My eldest daughter, Miranda, you were the first person to teach me the concept of selfless love; you have been a brilliant and courageous star in the lives of all you have touched for as long as I can remember. Robin Poett, my glorious wife, there are no words to describe the gift you are to me. This book and most of the beautiful things in my life would not exist without you! My love for you drives me to be a better man each and every day. To my younger daughters, Kayla and Rebecca, in your eyes and smiles I see hope for the future; you have brought more joy into my life than you can ever imagine, and ultimately that's what this book is all about!

To all the members of my creative team: Lori Buxton, my ever faithful and persistent partner, whose playful nagging helped turn "letters to my daughter" into the book you hold today. Michelle Peterson, my friend and mentor, who first took on the task of reining in my somewhat creative language and writing skills. My brilliant friend and editor James Donelan whose love of the written word and understanding of my coaching methods made this book a functional reality. And lastly, to Greg and Cynthia Sharp of Sea Hill Press for your belief in my vision and the love and effort you have poured into this work. I am so blessed to have all of you in my life!

Yours on this amazing adventure,

BILL POETT

CONTENTS

PREFACE

Ask with urgency and passion.

A. J. BALFOUR

"Why?" is a simple, powerful, and terrifying question. The answer to "Why?" has determined the fate of nations and driven our every action. Why am I here? Why do bad things happen to good people? Why should I exercise, study, open a savings account, or be kind to others? Why is God punishing me? Why am I so blessed? Living life well involves learning to answer these why questions in a way that empowers you.

Here is the why question you need to answer right now: why is this particular book in your hands? It is here to give you the keys to a new life. Each of the twenty-six chapters in this book represents a key to unlocking your potential through mental and emotional exercises, as if they opened onto a gym for your mind. This "Mind Gym" is the birthplace of imagination, wisdom, power, and potential. I will serve as your personal coach and guide. As you unlock and unleash your true potential, this book will aid you in designing, creating, and living the brilliant, beautiful, joy-filled life that is your birthright.

The reason you are holding this book is really very simple: you have decided to become empowered. As soon as you make that decision, like a magnet, you become drawn to the teachers, tools, and experiences you need to drive your life in the right direction. This book has appeared in your hands because it contains the information and coaching you need to find the answers to your life's biggest questions. If you are reading these words, you already know that you should be experiencing greater levels of joy, love, and success. We are having this conversation because you understand that with the right coach, training, and tools, your life will be better.

In other words, you found your way to this book because you have gotten stuck somewhere in your life's most important areas: career, relationships, and health. You've made it as far as you can with the way you usually do things. In order to experience greater levels of love, joy, and success, you need something new: a new coach!

As Albert Einstein (a peak performer if there ever was one) once said,

"We can't solve problems by using the same kind of thinking we used when we created them." Peak performers, regardless of their field of expertise, all have one thing in common: ongoing access to the best coaching and training in the world. To be world class in any endeavor—sports, business, health, or relationships—you need someone on your team, teaching, guiding, pulling, pushing, shouting, and cheering you on as you cross your goal line.

Now that you've decided that a great coach can help you experience a bigger, brighter, more joy-filled life, then the next question is: why Bill Poett? An excellent question! I, Bill Poett, am the best possible coach for you right now because I know how to win. More importantly, I know how to win in extreme situations, and I have spent the past twenty years teaching others to do the same thing. Let me show you what I mean through this scenario:

> On a cold, stormy night, you're driving home from a meeting downtown, and you've gotten lost. As you realize that you're in a dangerous part of the city, your engine begins to choke and sputter. You see the gas gauge on *E*, just as your motor takes its last breath and dies. As you curse yourself for having made so many mistakes, a brick crashes through the driver side window. Hands reach through the shattered glass and drag you from the car; you see light flashing on steel from the knife that is now speeding toward your heart!
>
> At this moment, winning is absolutely everything! The faces of your children fly across the screen of your mind, as the *blade heads toward its target. Without hesitation, you pivot* your torso ninety degrees, causing the blade to smash harmlessly into the car. Meanwhile, your elbow shatters your attacker's nose, as your rear hand traps his weapon. Your knee first strikes his groin, then his throat. You strip the knife from your attacker, as he collapses to the ground. With your attacker's weapon in your hand now, you watch him crawl, stagger, and finally run away. Assessing the situation, you see that you're safe for the moment, but you need to get out of here right now! You pull your emergency gas can from the trunk; you fuel up, and within thirty minutes you are safe and warm, back home in front of a fire. You're still trembling from the experience earlier in the evening, but as you walk down the hall and check on your wife and children, you make a pledge to yourself to prevent that kind of situation from happening again.

Please forgive me for guiding your imagination through this horrific chain of events, but this scenario will help you answer the very serious question you just asked yourself: why Bill Poett? As I said before, I know how to win, especially when winning matters most.

You see, before I became a performance coach, I spent over a decade as a close-quarter combat instructor. My specialty was knife fighting, and I had the privilege of teaching and training with some of America's most elite civilian, military, and law-enforcement teams. My job was to develop and teach peak performance skills to people whose jobs required them to face horrific, violent scenarios on a regular basis. They had to win because losing was unthinkable. Most players can lose and come back tomorrow to play again. Failure to my students would mean a trip to the hospital or the morgue. In the game we were playing, failure was literally not an option because failure meant serious injury or death.

You might ask now what a knife fighting instructor could possibly teach you in your relatively safe line of work. Once again, the answer is simple: everything! In close-quarter combat, a warrior relies on three assets to succeed and get home safely: body, mind, and spirit. To create the beautiful, joy-filled, successful life you desire, you will need the same three assets! I have spent a quarter century teaching people in combat, business, sports, and relationships how to win. I have tested and proven the value of these principles on all the various battlefields of life. I come to you today, committed, equipped, and prepared to help you develop the skills you need to experience a bigger, brighter, and more beautiful life.

Since 1988, I have been successfully teaching the art of winning through the systematic development of peak performance skills to thousands of men and women. The book you now hold in your hands will aid you in the development of twenty-six specific character traits or tools that are used by the world's best to achieve success in their lives. This is not a book of theory—the principles contained in each chapter have been tested and proven by me and countless others. The positive results you create from using this life guide will be directly proportional to the energy you invest in mastering each trait. With these tools, the success you have been seeking and the joys you have longed for are within your grasp. Peak performers are usually very ordinary men and women who possess extraordinary coaching, tools, and a desire to excel. I'll be your coach; together, we'll develop your tools. All you need is a burning desire to excel and the book you're holding in your hands.

HOW DO I SUCCEED?

We have answered the why question. Our next step involves looking at how we can get the most out of our time together? Like most "Keys" or "Secrets" to success, the answers to the how questions are fairly simple, but they do require work. With a committed effort on both our parts, and by using the tools contained in this book, we can and will create amazing results in your life. However, this book cannot and will not actually do anything for you, any more than a piece of gym equipment can do anything for you! This book, like any piece of equipment, is meant to be used by you to create the changes in your life you desire.

As your coach, I've designed the chapters, exercises, and mind workouts to be fun, challenging, and empowering, but like all successful training programs, the only way to produce consistent results is through consistent effort. I'll do my best to pull, push, and prod you to the finish line, but in the end, your efforts, not mine, will bring you the rewards you seek.

If I haven't scared you off yet with all this talk about work and commitment, then get ready, because it looks as if you have what it takes to become a peak performer. Peak performers expect and demand the best from themselves and others in order to get the greatest results possible from these twenty-six life lessons. I recommend you approach this adventure in building a brighter, more beautiful, joy-filled life in four steps:

1. **Dive In.** Read the book front to back, digesting all the Peak Performers Skills (PPS) A to Z. While this might sound obvious, it's vital to understand that the pathway up the "Peak Of Success" is littered with paid-for but unused gym memberships, exercise equipment, dusty and unread self-help and motivational books, and broken dreams, goals, marriages, businesses, and partnerships. No one ever sets out to quit, but quit they do, so here and now make a commitment to yourself and me, your coach, to read this book cover to

cover. I'm not asking for a huge commitment up front—this book has been designed to be the ideal weekend reading companion or an easy coast-to-coast read for you air travelers.

2. **Grade Yourself.** After reading each chapter, jump to pages 229-230 of the book, and give yourself a letter grade (A, B, C, D, F) for your current level of proficiency on every PPS. This is a purely subjective exercise, but it is essential if we are going to create positive results in your life as quickly as possible. An A grade would mean that this PPS is second nature, and it is a skill you use consistently, naturally, and without thought. Scoring a B would mean that you use this skill well and frequently, but you must actively focus on it. Cs are pretty much a wash—you have used the skill at times, but it is just as frequently missing. Grades of Ds and Fs are pretty self-explanatory. A note on grading: this form of personal inventory is extremely valuable and it will give you a pretty good snapshot of your strengths and weaknesses.

3. **Prioritize and Play.** Once you have finished the book and your Peak Performers Skill inventory, it's time for us to set up your training regimen. At this point, I need to emphasize that you are capable of developing any of these skills far beyond your imagining. In doing so, you will experience greater results, more consistent success, and deeper joys. Remember, like any other muscle or skill set, your PPS will improve with training and weaken when they are neglected.

My ultimate objective as your personal performance coach is to help you create a personalized training program that you will maintain and modify as needed for the rest of your life. The only thing sadder than a person who has never been fit and healthy is the athlete who has thrown away his or her strengths and skills out of laziness and neglect. On the page where you have graded your current skill sets, you'll see the column for training order. Having completed the book and graded yourself, you now want to set up your custom training program. Rank each PPS in order from 1 to 26, with the worst grade (the skill you need the most work on) as number 1.

4. **Train. Train. Train.** The fun begins. Each chapter should be studied "worst first." You have moved the skill sets you need the most to the top of your training schedule. Make the development of each chapter's skill a week-long project. Follow these steps:
   + Read the chapter and complete each assignment.
   + Place the word and definition at the top of each page in your calendar for the week.

+ Make notes on how the skill is used to create success around you.
+ Talk with family and friends about how using the skill has helped and how not using the skill has hurt.

This book is meant to be used, so please write in it, highlight it, and dog-ear it. Keep it handy, because you'll never know when you'll need of one of these chapters. Read it frequently, because as you grow in power, the lessons will take on new meaning. Read it with a friend, your spouse, or your kids. Do the exercises together, and you'll get even more out of it. Use it up, drink it in, and most importantly, let this book be a change driver in your life. Have fun with the lessons, play the game of life for all you're worth, but always remember: it's a game, and games are meant to be fun!

ABC LIFE RULES

As your performance coach, I would like you to read the "ABC Life Rules" before we begin training. They will serve as the foundation for the work we will be doing together and are meant to make your experience with this book as enjoyable and profitable as possible.

1. You are worthy! You deserve a beautiful, joy-filled life. Cultivating this belief is essential to becoming a peak performer.
2. Life's best is still ahead. Regardless of your age and previous life experience, with the right training and attitude, your today and tomorrow can be brighter than yesterday.
3. We are all interconnected. I can't hurt another person without hurting myself, or help another without helping myself.
4. Life is hard, but hard is not bad. Just as weight training helps us develop physical strength, and hard study helps us develop our intellects, adversity helps us develop our spirits.
5. If you're still here—that is, here on this planet, still alive—then you have always had everything you need.
6. Everyone gets the bad; you have to make the great happen. Live long enough and you will know the pain of loss, failure, and defeat. Only those who possess the courage to chase their dreams have a chance to know the great glories and the deep joys life has to offer.
7. Spend your life pursuing what you love—and if you don't know what you love, spend your life figuring it out. (I would have to call this one the golden rule of life's ABCs.)
8. Master the art of failing your way to the top. Unless you are willing to try and fail over and over again, you will never develop the skills you need to win the game of life.
9. Life is so serious; don't take yourself too seriously!

Welcome to the ABCs of peak performers!

INTRODUCTION

THE MAN WHO REMOVES A MOUNTAIN BEGINS BY
CARRYING AWAY SMALL STONES.

CHINESE PROVERB

Throughout this book, I will be sharing with you an alphabetical diet of ideas and life-enhancing techniques that can and will help you create positive change in your life—but there's a catch: Any tool or piece of information is valuable only when it is properly and consistently applied. The ABCs are meant to stimulate you to take action in your life. You'll find that different messages will have more impact on you at different times in your life. Remember, when the student is ready, the teacher will come. Don't give up, don't lose patience, and, please, consistently "play at being great."

As for your coach, there is nothing particularly remarkable about me, and I am certainly not taking credit for creating any of this great stuff. These techniques and this information have been around a long time. I'm as fallible as anybody—I fail more often than I succeed, but you won't hear me complain a lot. When I get knocked down, I always get up quickly, and I'll be the first to apologize when I realize I have done or said something stupid, which can be frequently—just ask my wife. The messenger is only human, so look at the message instead.

Now as Hatsumi Sensei, one of my greatest teachers, would say before any important lesson, "Let's play!"

A
<u>ATTITUDE</u>

1. Your physical, mental, and emotional posture (state), as you interpret and react to all of the events—both real and imagined—unfolding in your life.

GOOD, BAD; POSITIVE, NEGATIVE; INSPIRED, UNMOTIVATED—
OUR ATTITUDES ARE THE COLORS WITH WHICH
WE PAINT THE CANVAS OF OUR LIVES.

As a warrior, I was trained to believe and demonstrate that attitude is everything; as a pilot, I learned the same thing. Like many children, I was frequently told when I was young that I needed to improve my attitude. What is attitude? What does it mean? How do we use and develop it? Helping you answer these questions is what this book is all about.

This isn't an easy concept to wrap your head around, yet I'm sure you've heard about the importance of a "good attitude" and the dangers of a "bad attitude" your entire life. How often have you heard a parent or spouse say he or she didn't like your "attitude"? As scary as it sounds, this thing called attitude is a beautiful and terrible beast that, when understood, tamed, and managed effectively, can lead us to a life of joy and abundance. But when it is not respected and is left running wild, it can be a primary cause of our misery.

The problem is that most of what makes up our attitude is not of our creation, and getting control of it is one of the great challenges on the quest for peak performance. Your attitude today comes from a combination of your DNA, environment, parental and societal programming, and God knows what else. Tides, stars, hormones, the stock market have all been tossed into this karmic stew! Think of your attitude as the software you use to understand, interpret, and interact with the world around you. I hate to be the bearer of bad news, but there are some big bugs in your software. Understanding these bugs will explain a lot about what isn't working in your life and your world!

Attitude bugs occur when you think the following:

+ I am not worthy.
+ I could never do that.
+ It's too hard.
+ It's not my fault.
+ It's not my responsibility.
+ Why do bad things always happen to me?
+ I don't have enough …

The examples are endless, and when you find yourself consistently struggling with depression, lack of motivation, and poor performance, you can look to bugs in your attitude as driving these physical, emotional, and mental states.

The great news is that you have the power, ability, and ultimately the responsibility to rewrite your personal software. Peak performers make attitude management a priority in their lives. For that, they are rewarded with great energy, motivation, enthusiasm, and ultimately, more joy, less stress, and greater achievement. Creating and sustaining a positive attitude requires a lifetime of mindful action. To do that, you need to create a physical environment along with an educational and emotional support system that constantly reinforces the changes in attitude you are seeking.

Why? Because people whose professions require peak performance in life-or-death situations, such as pilots and warriors, must control their attitudes. Pilots use the word *attitude* to mean the plane's position relative to the air (a combination of the plane's motion and the wind) and to the ground. That's because the plane's attitude represents its primary relationship with its environment. An experienced pilot can change his plane's attitude in response to atmospheric conditions and his desired destination. If you don't have that attitude under control, your plane will crash—and everything else is secondary to that one fact.

A warrior's attitude is just as important. His attitude is his emotional, intellectual, and physical relationship with his assailant, and once he has that under control, he can do anything. An experienced warrior can change his attitude in response to his assailant's energy or mode of attack. If you can keep your attitude under control and put it to work for you, you can conquer anyone or anything!

Attitude at Work

When you grow up on a ranch, you learn a lot about attitude at a pretty early age. When my daughter Miranda was eleven, she wanted to ride her horse, Amber Lee, on her first time gathering cattle, although they were both pretty inexperienced. Reluctantly, I agreed to let her do this. We'd been out for a couple of hours, and they were doing a great job, both of them showing a natural cow sense and enjoying each other's company, as they learned how to do their jobs.

We had finished moving the cattle and were on our way home when we came up to a creek. Some horses can get a little nervous around water, and neither this tired horse nor its tired rider felt like crossing it, but we had to because that's how we get home. Amber Lee started to hop around a bit, and Miranda was getting really scared. Remember, horses are massive animals and do what we want primarily because they trust us, so a scared horse and a scared rider are dangerous. I could tell that unless both the horse and its rider made a serious attitude adjustment, they were going to get hurt.

At first, Miranda wanted to get off and quit riding, but quitting when things get a little rough was not a lesson I wanted her to learn that day. I rode right up alongside her and got my face about a foot from hers, looked her straight in the eye, and quietly said—in a pretty good Clint Eastwood voice—"Ride that horse across this creek right now." I didn't blink or move, but her eyes got really big, then they focused hard, as she turned toward the creek. In a voice that projected total confidence, she said "COME ON" and gave Amber Lee a little kick. Over the creek they went, and she turned back and looked at me. I got to witness the biggest, most beautiful grin spread across her face. It must have been contagious because I found myself wearing exactly the same grin. She had changed her attitude in an instant and conquered her fear. She had also learned a lesson about the power of attitude that has followed her through every challenge she has faced ever since, and there have been plenty.

I HAD THE BLUES BECAUSE I HAD NO SHOES UNTIL UPON THE STREET,
I MET A MAN WHO HAD NO FEET.

ANCIENT PERSIAN SAYING

Growing Attitude

Most people live in a reactive state (outside-in); their attitudes are determined by a limitless array of uncontrollable events taking place in the world around them. They move through life on an emotional roller-coaster with everything from the weather to the stock market controlling their moods as well as their performance. Peak performers are experts at managing their environment and their attitudes; they understand that they can't control all of the events taking place around them, but they are in absolute control of how they act in relation to them. This inside-out approach to life is key to experiencing consistent success in an ever changing world. What's our lesson from this story? First, manage your environment.

MANAGE YOUR ENVIRONMENT.

We become what surrounds us, and as the programmers say, garbage in—garbage out. Every sight, sound, comment, noise, news report, family member, friend, and associate has an impact on our attitude. Surround yourself with beauty, positive images, whole foods, nature's wonders, and powerful, enthusiastic people, and you will be hard pressed to maintain a "bad attitude." Miranda was ready to change her attitude in response to a challenging situation because she had been raised in a sound environment: a ranch with good animals, good people, and every other positive environmental factor that ranch life gives you. When her challenge came, she had eleven years of experience watching other people face up to challenges instead of backing down. A sound environment—and a little push from her father—was all she needed.

Managing your environment is trickier than it sounds. A great teacher once said, "To find enlightenment alone in a cave is easy. If you can find enlightenment in a home filled with noisy children, unpaid bills, an irritated spouse, and a broken toilet—then, you have found the true path." But your environment will always have something negative in it—that's just part of life. Even if it were possible to insulate yourself completely from negative people, events, and surroundings, you wouldn't want to do it. Many of your greatest teachers and opportunities come in the form of adversity. Struggles in your relationships, business, and environment help develop and strengthen you. An ancient Japanese proverb teaches us, "The hotter the flame, the sharper the sword." Or as mom and dad would say, "Don't worry; it builds character." Mom and dad were right—and what they meant by "character" is the power to manage your attitude.

You need to create and maintain a sound environment during times of both peace and conflict. Doing so will determine how well you handle life's challenges, opportunities, and disasters. Everybody handles the good stuff well. We define ourselves by how we handle the bad.

Upgrade your machine.

I am amazed at how many of us are convinced that we must upgrade our computers, TVs, and cars every few years, when we rarely utilize or use up the value of what we now own. While we are shopping for the newest, fastest, most powerful computer, we are neglecting to upgrade our most powerful machine: ourselves! Twenty years of martial arts taught me one profound lesson: The gun, the knife, and the club aren't really weapons—they are merely tools. You are the weapon, and your effectiveness in the completion of any task is determined almost exclusively by the mental, emotional, and physical skills you develop.

Your ability to manage your attitude and handle life's challenges is in direct proportion to the mental, emotional, and physical powers you bring with you daily. It's essential that you create a weekly training protocol that strengthens your body, mind, and spirit. This performance maintenance program should consist of:

+ Weekly exercise, proper nutrition, and hydration (a lot of water every day)

- ◆ Continuing education in your career: classes, books, trade journals …
- ◆ Ongoing study of human performance skill sets
- ◆ Visualization, meditation, and prayer

The key to this performance maintenance program is not volume, but consistency. Four hours of exercise, four hours of education, and two hours of reflection, visualization, and prayer will have a greater positive impact on your attitude then you can possibly imagine.

This ten hour investment in your attitude and personal development requires about a third as much time as the average American spends in front of the television.

PRACTICE DAILY FORGIVENESS AND THANKSGIVING.

You are not perfect; you have not been designed to be. Your upbringing wasn't perfect either, and the choices, decisions, and actions you make every day won't be. Learn to love who and where you are. If you can find joy at this point in your evolution, it will make it so much easier to progress along whatever path you choose. We don't judge babies harshly because they can't walk and talk, yet they're exactly where they should be. Learn to make allowances for the different levels of mental, emotional, and spiritual development that we experience. Forgive yourself every day when you fail to live up to the "ideal you." This doesn't mean that you should lower your standards, make excuses, or blame others. It simply means that when you fall short of your expectations, then learn from your mistakes, dust yourself off, and do it again. The best batters in the history of baseball failed six out of ten times at bat. As you find self-forgiveness coming to you more easily, your ability to forgive others will expand as well.

You are a miracle. I love birthdays because I love thinking of all of the millions of seemingly random events that had to occur to bring each of us into existence. I love watching people learn, play, work, and study. When you really think about the fact that you can receive information from a book or a computer, read it, understand it, and then act on it, you can see how amazing we really are! I can't help but say it again: you are a miracle. I know your back hurts, and you don't look exactly like an underwear model, and you don't have all of the money, time, and things you want. But you are here, you are in the game, you can love, and you are loved. You can learn and play and laugh and cry. There is nothing quite as beautiful anywhere else in the universe.

Spend time each day being thankful for all the things that you do have instead of feeling bad about those you don't. Every piece of knowledge that has ever been recorded is here now for your benefit. All of the art, literature, poetry, and film are here now for your entertainment. The world is teeming with people wanting to learn, love, and laugh with you. Every sunset, sunrise, ocean, star, mountain, and flower has been placed on this planet for you to enjoy and appreciate. It is impossible to self-loathe and maintain a positive attitude, just as it is impossible to love the miracle that you are and maintain a negative attitude.

The amount of JOY you manifest over the course of your life is in direct proportion to your ability to acknowledge and celebrate the miracle that is YOU! Thanks for playing, and enjoy exercising your attitude management techniques. Discuss them with your family and friends. And most importantly, be great—the world needs you!

IF YOU WILL CALL YOUR TROUBLES EXPERIENCES, AND REMEMBER THAT EVERY EXPERIENCE DEVELOPS SOME LATENT FORCE WITHIN YOU, YOU WILL GROW VIGOROUS AND HAPPY, HOWEVER ADVERSE YOUR CIRCUMSTANCES MAY BE.

JOHN HEYWOOD

Attitude Exercises

EXERCISE 1.

Right now, grab a pen and write down the first ten gifts that you are thankful for. These can be people, skills, or objects of beauty. It's your life, and there are no limits to the things you may enjoy. Do it every day this week, and never use the same thing twice. Don't get up until you have recorded at least ten. This is the beginning of learning to live within an attitude of gratitude.

1. _____
2. _____
3. _____
4. _____
5. _____
6. _____
7. _____
8. _____
9. _____
10. _____

EXERCISE 2.

Walk through your home and office examining each item, then review your weekly calendar, address book, and contact list to see how you spend your time at work and at play, and most importantly, with whom you spend it. Now mentally place a large plus, minus, or zero next to each item, activity, and individual according to the scheme below. You can start with three items a day or thirty, but what matters is that you do this consistently until it becomes a habit.

+ *Mark with a plus (+):* Items, activities, and individuals that add to your joy, health, knowledge, and function. Your life is brighter, less stressful, more productive, and happier because these items, activities, and individuals are a part of it. Surround yourself with as many pluses as possible. These serve to feed your light and energy and positively drive your attitude.

+ *Mark with a minus (–):* Items, activities, and individuals that cause stress, clutter, negative habits, and unhealthy patterns. Get rid of them whenever possible. These are life vampires and they will suck out your light, energy, and ability to handle adversity. When you are forced to deal with them, surround yourself with a mental shield, complete the interaction as quickly as possible, and leave without letting their negative energy follow you. This takes mindful practice, but the payoff in protecting your positive attitude is huge.

- *Mark with a zero (0)*: Items, activities, and individuals that don't necessarily add to or detract from the quality of your life. However, you should keep in mind that because we live in a culture of consumption, these kinds of items surround you. Closets, garages, storage units, and daily calendars are full of them. They add clutter and expense to our lives; they are time and resource stealers, so get rid of them. Have a garage sale, learn how to use eBay, or donate them to your favorite charity. You'll have less stress and more money almost immediately. For peak performers, less is more.

If

If you can keep your head when all about you
Are losing theirs and blaming it on you,
If you can trust yourself when all men doubt you,
But make allowance for their doubting too;
If you can wait and not be tired by waiting,
Or being lied about, don't deal in lies,
Or being hated, don't give way to hating,
And yet don't look too good, nor talk too wise:

If you can dream—and not make dreams your master;
If you can think—and not make thoughts your aim;
If you can meet with Triumph and Disaster
And treat those two imposters just the same;
If you can bear to hear the truth you've spoken
Twisted by knaves to make a trap for fools,
Or watch the things you gave your life to, broken,
And stoop and build 'em up with worn-out tools:

If you can make one heap of all your winnings
And risk it on one turn of pitch-and-toss,
And lose, and start again at your beginnings
And never breath a word about your loss;
If you can force your heart and nerve and sinew
To serve your turn long after they are gone,
And so hold on when there is nothing in you
Except the Will which says to them: "Hold on!"

If you can talk with crowds and keep your virtue,
Or walk with Kings—nor lose the common touch,
If neither foes nor loving friends can hurt you,
If all men count with you, but none too much;
If you can fill the unforgiving minute
With sixty seconds' worth of distance run,
Yours is the Earth and everything that's in it,
And—which is more—you'll be a Man, my son!

RUDYARD KIPLING

B
<u>BALANCE</u>

The ability to maintain physical, mental, and emotional equilibrium while under pressure from external forces.

BALANCE IS A FUNNY THING—WITHOUT IT NO-THING IS POSSIBLE; WITH IT MOST THINGS CAN BE ACHIEVED. AND YET, IT IS A MOMENT THAT WE CAN ONLY TOUCH AND NEVER OWN. IN THIS LIFE, YOU WILL NOT BE JUDGED BY HOW MANY TIMES YOU STUMBLE AND FALL, BUT BY THE SPEED WITH WHICH YOU GET BACK UP AGAIN.

I LIKE TO tell people this parable about balance: I once knew a man who lived for success in his career. He worked, sacrificed, and spent his life climbing the corporate ladder. Along the way, his ambition hurt his relationship with his family and broke down his health. He became forty pounds overweight; he took pills for his blood pressure and high cholesterol; but with the help of his therapist—and a little scotch—he managed to make it through each day. After forty years of struggle, constantly fighting, biting, and clawing his way up, he finally made it to the top. He took a breath of this beautiful fresh air (remember, it's better up there) and looked around. He thought to himself, yes, the view is great up here. He was so excited that he couldn't wait to share the news with the people he loved the most, but they were gone. Suddenly, painfully, and with great clarity, he realized that the ladder he had spent his entire life climbing was leaning against the wrong wall.

Almost all human fears are taught, but we fear falling instinctively. That's why so much of the first four years of our lives are spent learning how to balance. In the beginning, we struggle simply to stand; then we begin walking and running, until we find it so easy that we can play without thinking about it. This gift of balance can lead us to the Olympics or to an office in the executive suite of a large company. But the universe, in its infinite wisdom, understands the importance of balance far better than we do, and we ignore the dangers of losing balance at our peril.

Keeping your balance will keep you safe from more than accidents. As a close-quarter combat instructor, I learned that it was impossible to prepare my students for every potential threat, so instead of focusing on techniques or tricks, I taught them principles that apply to all combat scenarios—especially balance. Remove an opponent's physical, mental, or emotional balance and you have begun to neutralize the threat. Lose your physical, mental, or emotional balance in combat and recovery will be next to impossible.

The happiest and most successful individuals are those who consistently demonstrate exceptional life-balancing skills. Human beings are multifaceted, and that's a beautiful thing, but balancing all the roles we're expected to play is difficult. Calling each role that we assume a "hat" is a common expression with a lot of truth in it. We have our parent hat, our child hat, our teacher hat, and our student hat. We have our lover hat, our business hat, our friend hat, and our cat hat. All right, maybe only Dr. Seuss has a cat hat, but you get the point. We are many different things to many different people.

The real issue is how those hats have multiplied. As society moves faster and becomes more specialized, we have taken on more roles than at any other time in history. But taking on more roles will not necessarily give you a healthier, happier life. Imagine being a circus plate juggler whose assistant doesn't know when to stop handing him more plates. Regardless of how skilled the juggler is, he becomes more and more frantic as the number of plates increase, until, inevitably, he can't juggle any more, and broken plates are everywhere. Stephen Covey once made a great point about the difference between being efficient and being effective. An efficient person gets a lot done—he juggles a lot of plates. An effective person gets the right thing done—he is very cautious about adding and managing plates, and he rarely drops any. Effective people maintain balance in their lives, and they do it every day.

How can you maintain balance? First, you should realize that the art of balance is really about time. It is the one asset that, once spent, can never be reclaimed. Our lives take place in the element of time—when we paint the moments of our lives, time is our canvas. Peak performers find that with twenty-four-hour days and seven-day weeks, we have ample time to devote to each important role in our lives. However, we guard our time very carefully, knowing that the limits of our time, energy, and attention are always there, and that these limits change constantly. Our physical, mental, and emotional health affects our ability to manage our roles, and these factors are affected by a number of environmental factors. With all these forces at work, balance isn't easy—but it's essential.

Balance at Work

In a perfect world, a single twenty-four-hour day would be divided into three equal parts. We would work for eight hours at something we love doing or, at the very least, at something that we cared about deeply. We would have eight hours for recreation, or as I like to call it, re-creation—that is, creating ourselves anew. This time would include playing with family and friends, exercising, and participating in any other activity that refreshes, inspires, relaxes, and brings us joy. Then we would sleep for eight hours. During our seven-day week, we would budget time for important activities in each sphere of our life that means something to us: ourselves, our family, our friends, and society in general. Daily and weekly, we would reflect on how well we were balancing our important roles and make adjustments accordingly.

So DIVINELY IS THE WORLD ORGANIZED THAT EVERY ONE OF US, IN OUR PLACE AND TIME, IS IN BALANCE WITH EVERYTHING ELSE.

JOHANN WOLFGANG VON GOETHE

Growing Balance

There's a big difference between ideal models and the real world. I like to think about this difference with something I learned from close-quarter combat training. We call it the "dojo syndrome." Basically, it's the difference between what happens in training and what it's like to do something out there in the real world. Most martial arts students in America practice stylized attacks on perfect surfaces with friendly faces. These make-believe fights look nothing like what actually takes place out in what we call "the mud, blood, and beer," that is, the uncontrolled, unexpected circumstances where most violence takes place. (If you knew where violence was going to be, you'd avoid it, wouldn't you?) Far too many college courses and business models have the same problem. They bear little resemblance to what our young men and women are finding in the real world, and they assume ideal conditions that rarely occur in reality.

How do peak performers overcome dojo syndrome? They keep balance in mind and strive to maintain it, and when they can't stay in balance, they find ways to reclaim it. Military people call it training for "snafus" and "fubars," which are essentially the two main categories in which things go wrong in a military environment. *Snafu* is short for "situation normal, all f---ed up," that is, when there is a structural problem that will always throw you off balance. For example, when five thousand men get off a ship all at once in the same place, there is inevitably going to be confusion. People and things get lost, connections are missed, and everything takes longer than it should. The point is that staying focused, organized, and on task is always hard; normal conditions tend toward chaos. That's life, and you need to leave time and energy for it.

Fubar, on the other hand, is short for "f---ed up beyond all recognition," the general military term for a situation in which something has changed dramatically. When you think you have a sound, stable structure in which to accomplish a task, you find that something essential has been absolutely ruined or isn't there. You're supposed to report to a command post, for instance, and it's been blown apart by artillery, or it was moved, or it was never set up in the first place, and no one told you anything. The situation is fubar—so what do you do now?

These kinds of things happen all the time in combat, and good military people find ways to handle them. Snafus will occur when you have massive logistical issues, changing conditions and objectives, and a lot of people and things that need to get done. When the action starts—and often, even before—a whole lot of plans, people, and things will be fubar. But here's the big question: can you find balance in your life when life sends you the usual snafus? Better yet, can you regain your balance when things in your life actually become fubar?

Yes, you can, but you have to learn to fall first. Fighting against an overwhelming force leads ultimately to exhaustion, frustration, and defeat. Learning how to ride and guide an overwhelming force leads to movement, flow, and victory. In martial arts, you can reach a point where choosing to fall in a controlled manner is much more effective then struggling to stay upright. There will be times in our lives when we have to make the same choice. That means mindfully living out of balance. No one has a child or starts a new business or career without losing balance. Both of these babies need almost all of our waking focus and attention. When we make these huge changes well and enlist the support of our family and friends, the payoff is huge. Few satisfactions are as great as watching your children move into the world and begin contributing and performing on their own. Giving birth to an idea or a business that you believe in and taking it from concept to production is another of life's great rewards. But to do something this great, you're going to have to fall down a few times, then get back up and into balance again.

Think about those falls, plan for them the best you can, and deal with them when they happen. The trap lies in getting stuck in the comfort of any particular role. Sure, the mom or businessperson role can give you many rewards, but if you're too stuck in one of those roles, you may neglect the other important roles in your life, leading to a permanent state of un-balance and life failure.

These exercises will help you to determine where your life is out of balance, to schedule balance solutions, and to commit to taking action and moving your life forward. Remember, be great—the world needs you!

THE BEST AND SAFEST THING IS TO KEEP A BALANCE IN YOUR LIFE,
ACKNOWLEDGE THE GREAT POWERS AROUND US AND IN US.
IF YOU CAN DO THAT, AND LIVE THAT WAY, YOU ARE REALLY A WISE MAN.

EURIPIDES

Balance Exercises

EXERCISE 1.

We are going to take a snapshot of your life and allow you a moment to examine your current state of balance. Think of this as a life inventory. Be honest in your evaluation; remember, feedback is the breakfast of champions. Don't get frustrated—the idea is to get some information to find out where you are and to help you manage these issues, not to bog you down. Give each category an A through F grade.

_____ Physical: balance, strength, cardio endurance, muscle tone, energy level, and sports function.

_____ Mental: education, problem solving, creativity, imagination, and discipline.

_____ Emotional: ability to handle stress, relationships, confidence, and joy.

_____ Family/friends: positive, healthy, and honest relationships with the people you care about the most.

_____ Service/community/societal: contribution above and beyond your immediate circle of influence.

EXERCISE 2.

Review your grades from the previous exercise, and highlight every category that received a grade of C or below. Take a moment, breathe, and open yourself up to the self-knowledge that we all posses. Ask yourself the following question: what is one action I can take this week in each of these categories that will improve my grade? Write the answers below.

EXERCISE 3.

Action, Action, Action! Take out your day planner and select one of the actions from the previous exercise. Write your action steps into your calendar. Remember, knowledge is not power—accurate, applied action is power!

The goal of these ABCs is to get you to take small, consistent action each week. The idea is not to take big bites, but little ones. Think of it this way: by making a 2 percent weekly improvement in the quality of the choices you make, the actions you take will literally transform everything about your life experience. Think of it as compound interest on the quality of your life!

All the World's a Stage

All the world's a stage,
And all the men and women merely players;
They have their exits and their entrances,
And one man in his time plays many parts,
His acts being seven ages. At first, the infant,
Mewling and puking in the nurse's arms.
Then the whining schoolboy, with his satchel
And shining morning face, creeping like a snail
Unwillingly to school. And then the lover,
Sighing like furnace, with a woeful ballad
Made to his mistress' eyebrow. Then a soldier,
Full of strange oaths and bearded like the pard,
Jealous in honor, sudden and quick in quarrel,
Seeking the bubble reputation
Even in the cannon's mouth. And then the justice,
In fair round belly with good capon lined,
With eyes severe and beard of formal cut,
Full of wise saws and modern instances;
And so he plays his part. The sixth age shifts
Into the lean and slippered pantaloon,
With spectacles on nose and pouch on side;
His youthful hose, well saved, a world too wide
For his shrunk shank, and his big manly voice,
Turning again toward childish treble, pipes
And whistles in his sound. Last scene of all,
That ends this strange eventful history,
Is second childishness and mere oblivion,
Sans teeth, sans eyes, sans taste, sans everything.

WILLIAM SHAKESPEARE

C
<u>CONFIDENCE</u>

*1. Acting on your potential. 2. Knowing you can achieve a goal
completely outside your realm of experience.*

IT DOESN'T MATTER IF YOU ARE PREDATOR OR PREY—WHEN YOU WAKE UP,
YOU HAD BETTER HAVE THE CONFIDENCE TO RUN!

TALK TO ANY skydiver and he will tell you that the hundredth jump doesn't take confidence, the first one does! Confidence is much more than a belief. It is acting on your unharnessed potential and moving beyond the safety of things you know. Starting a new business, asking that beautiful girl on a date (or saying "yes" when asked), making your first black diamond ski run, leaving your job to raise your children—these are all acts that require confidence.

Confidence at Work

We are surrounded by examples of confidence in action: world class athletes, successful businesspeople, and creative, engaged, loving parents are everywhere. The fastest way to develop proficiency and confidence in any field of endeavor is modeling, that is, by imitating others. Find the best people in the world (remember, no limits!) at something you want to do well, and become a human sponge. Absorb every piece of information you can find about the actions, beliefs, and practices of your selected peak performer. Begin implementing them in your life immediately. There is truth in the expression, "Fake it till you make it." Act like a peak performer, and you will become one yourself!

We have more direct access to peak performers than at any time in history. Twenty years ago, when I really began pursuing my martial arts training in earnest, I was forced to travel all over the country to get access to the best instructors in the world. Today, these men and women have websites, books, and videos providing immediate access to the best information available. You can bring these coaches right into your living room with a few clicks on your keyboard. The world's best yoga instructors, business coaches, tennis instructors, and chefs are waiting to share a lifetime of knowledge with you.

Master instructors of any craft are committed to bringing you to greater levels of performance and to saving you countless hours of repeating the mistakes they made along the way. There might be a cost of time and money when you pursue expert instruction, but it is nothing in comparison with the time and money you will spend trying to reinvent the wheel. Remember the adage, "If you think education is expensive, try ignorance." Don't forget to look right in your backyard for experts; you would be amazed at how many great minds there are that would love nothing more than to pass on their knowledge. When I first started out in the martial arts business, I contacted the owner of one of the most successful schools in the United States. His name was Jeff Smith, and he was out of Washington, D.C. After several communications, he invited me to come to D.C. and shadow him for a week. Three years later, my first dojo was named a top one hundred school in the United States.

You never know what resources are available to you until you ask. When it became time for me to franchise my business, I discovered that the founder of the International House of Pancakes restaurant chain was the grandfather of one of my students; again, with nothing more than a request, I was able to set up weekly business coaching sessions with him at no cost.

OUR DOUBTS ARE TRAITORS, AND MAKE US LOSE THE GOOD WE OFT MIGHT WIN, BY FEARING TO ATTEMPT.

WILLIAM SHAKESPEARE

Growing Confidence

Every quality or skill we discuss here in the *ABCs* can be developed using the same techniques we use to develop muscle mass and strength in the gym. Muscle mass is achieved by exposing different muscle groups to *negative stimulation*, in this case, weight training. Weight training creates small tears in muscle tissue, which after an essential (and too often ignored) period of rest and proper nutrition, causes the body to adapt and rebuild the damaged tissue into better, stronger, and more functional muscle. Our intellect, character, and confidence are all developed using the same cycle of negative stimulation and adaptive response. The reason that more people don't have healthy, beautiful, highly functional, bodies, minds, and spirits is simple: negative stimulation hurts!

No one is born with the ability to run a four-minute mile, get into a top university, or do a flip on a balance beam. And, yet, these world class achievements have been accomplished by men and women possessing the same basic tools you and I possess. The achievers differ from us in that they take consistent action to maximize their own potential. World class performance is developed through thousands of hours of practice, study, and training, all of which involve some kind of negative stimulation.

You can grow your confidence by consistently forcing yourself outside your comfort zone into an area of negative stimulation, until, like a muscle, your confidence expands to meet the new loads place on it.

In 1980, I was failing speech. It was one of those general elective classes I had absolutely no interest in, and it was after rodeo practice, when I usually had horse crap on my Wranglers. My plan was to attend every class, do well on all the written tests, and avoid giving a speech entirely. I figured I could squeak through with a C- and move on with my life. Like many people, I found the thought of thirty pairs of strangers' eyes staring at me while I spoke terrifying. So, I followed the plan. I showed up to class every day—except for presentation days—passed all the written tests, and finished the class with a well-deserved F. My fear of public speaking wasn't conquered; it was reinforced by my avoidance of negative stimulation.

The same year, I was invited to try a class at a friend's martial arts school and fell in love with the training. I've always been fairly athletic, and there was something beautiful about the martial arts philosophy and its emphasis on body control and self-development that completely swept me up. During my first year of training, I skipped two belt levels and was asked to become an assistant instructor. My responsibilities included directing the class warm-up and basic exercises and providing technical assistance for the new students. I'll never forget my first evening in my new assistant instructor's uniform. I stood on the side of the mat getting ready to bow class in. There were probably twelve to fifteen adults of varying levels, and I was terrified. I kept wiping sweat from my hands on the side of my uniform, and I couldn't stop clearing my throat. I was sure every student knew how nervous I was. I did everything I had rehearsed in my mind. I faked confidence as best I could, and after class, I got a ton of positive feedback. I was elated. I continued teaching three or four nights a week.

For at least the first one hundred classes, I had that "Oh my god I'm gonna puke feeling" meet me at the door. But something wonderful started to happen: I realized that the feeling didn't seem to hang around as long as it used to. Then, one day, it simply stopped. My comfort zone had expanded, and what was once terrifying had now become easy. More importantly, I understood the process.

Over the next ten years, my teaching expanded from traditional martial arts to business management, executive leadership, and team building. Ten years after my failed speech class, I was invited to be a keynote speaker at a convention in Fort Lauderdale. There were well over one thousand people in the audience, and because of the size of the crowd, the promoters were using a forty-foot video screen behind the stage. As I prepped behind the screen, I did a palm check (clammy, which is good), cleared my throat (dry, also good), and smiled to myself. I knew I was going to knock this one out of the park, and I did! Not bad for a kid too terrified to speak.

FAILING YOUR WAY TO CONFIDENCE.

"Failing" is one of the most misunderstood words in the English language, and if I were king, I'd outlaw it and replace it with "feedback." The average overnight success takes twenty years to arrive, and performance experts have come up with ten thousand as the number of hours it takes to become a master of any field of endeavor. Babe Ruth, one of the greatest sluggers in the history of baseball, will always be remembered for his home run record. What has already been forgotten is that during the same period, the "Babe" struck out more than any other major league player. When Thomas Edison was interviewed about his startling success in inventing the light bulb, he said that there was nothing startling about it. After over one thousand failed experiments, he simply had run out of ways to fail. Success was inevitable. Every time we take an action that doesn't produce our expected result, we are one step closer to success.

We hear about fear of failure all the time, but I'm convinced that there's really nothing to be afraid of. There are only two situations where failure is possible, and neither can occur unless you allow it to happen. The first occurs when you have a desire and take no action on it; the second occurs when you begin pursuing a goal and quit after a perceived failure, that is, when you fail to put negative feedback to good use. The only time you're guaranteed to fail is when you never try or stop trying too soon.

THEY CAN BECAUSE THEY THINK THEY CAN.

VIRGIL

Confidence Exercises

EXERCISE 1.

Confidence is most easily developed by continuous upgrades of the machine, and you are the machine. In our last two sections, we looked at the importance of a balanced approach to your personal development. Right now, give yourself an honest appraisal of how well you have followed through on your weekly training by giving yourself a grade for last week's performance in each of the following categories:

_____ Physical Development (four hours per week of exercise is an A)
_____ Intellectual Development (four hours per week of class, research, or study is an A)
_____ Emotional/Spiritual Development (two hours per week of service, meditation, visualization, goal setting, and prayer is an A)

Then write down one activity you can do this week to improve your weekly diet of personal development!

EXERCISE 2.

Modeling for confidence requires selecting one of your stretch goals, something you have always dreamed of becoming, doing, or having. Find two resources: one material and one human.

- The first will be a teaching tool: website, class, DVD, book, or tape.
- The other should be a mentor with whom you can speak personally, one who excels in your chosen field of endeavor.

EXERCISE 3.

Take immediate action by scheduling your personal development activities for the upcoming week.

- Order your teaching/modeling material.
- Find and make contact with a mentor, teacher, or coach.

If you're still reading this, then you fall into the top 10 percent of men and women truly committed to building a happier, more beautiful, successful life. Thank you for investing this time in your growth and development. You are one of the bright lights in a world that too often seems dark!

Thinking

If you think you are beaten, you are
If you think you dare not, you don't,
If you like to win but think you can't
It's almost a cinch you won't.

If you think you'll lose, you're lost
For out in the world we find,
Success begins with a fellow's will
It's all in the state of mind.

If you think you are outclassed, you are
You've got to think high to rise,
You've got to be sure of yourself before
You can ever win the prize.

Life's battles don't always go
To the stronger or faster man,
But sooner or later, the man who wins
Is the man who thinks he can!

WALTER D. WINTLE

D
DISCIPLINE

Doing what needs to be done, when it needs to be done, regardless of what you want to do!

SOME HEAR THE WORD DISCIPLINE AND THINK OF PUNISHMENT; I HEAR THE WORD DISCIPLINE AND THINK OF POWER.

MY DAUGHTER BECCA, at sixteen months old, loved building blocks. Once, we were playing in her room, and as I watched her, I thought about how I have used my blocks over the years. I believe at birth we are all given a bagful of blocks. Everyone's bag is different, in both the quantity and the quality of blocks it contains. These blocks represent our advantages and our disadvantages, and despite what the Founding Fathers said about all men being created equal, it's not true when it comes to these blocks. (Jefferson and the rest of them meant equality in terms of fundamental political rights, not equality of ability, but that's another story.) Each one of us is blessed, at birth, with our own unique gifts and obstacles—our blocks—and no two sets are equal! As a performance coach or, more accurately, a student of great achievers, I have been humbled, awed, and often frustrated by the amazing things I have seen men and women create in their lives, frequently with a block set much smaller than mine. Ultimately, the quality of our lives has little to do with our talents and potential (blocks) and everything to do with what we create with them.

Looks, intellect, education, parenting, money, physical prowess, emotional stability, and environment are only some of the blocks that come in our bag. If you look at the lives of some great achievers—Albert Einstein, Mother Teresa, Bill Gates, Nelson Mandela, Magic Johnson, and Neil Armstrong—you'll discover that these peak performers rarely have everything they need as children, or even as adults. The world changers are not those with the most gifts, but rather those who do the most with what they have. What every one of them does have is vitally important: discipline.

Discipline at Work

If confidence is the foundation of all achievement, then discipline is the elbow grease. Discipline enables us to transform our dreams into realities. It is one of the most vital and least sexy of all our skill sets. Discipline is not generally something we get excited about, but it's what makes things happen. It's putting one foot in front of the other; it's the twelve-hour work day; it's burning out the last three reps of a set at the gym; it's making one more cold call or putting in those extra hours at the library, when all of your friends are out partying. Discipline is a relentless, focused effort, carried on without fail until the job is done.

Over the years, I have had the opportunity to train with members of our nation's top military and civilian special response teams. These men and women place themselves in harm's way for our protection. Their work is dangerous, even when they do everything well. Consequently, special response teams have no tolerance for mediocrity. In their world, a less than stellar performance can cost lives, so they select and train their team members for peak performance. Their work requires levels of discipline and training that border on the fanatic because, in combat, the lag time between choice and consequence is almost nonexistent and delay can be lethal. These people do what needs to be done, when it needs to be done, each and every day, so that they can get the job done and come home alive and well.

Most of us will never know what it's like to cover someone's back as they take down a door, fight a wildfire, or give first aid to disaster victims, but all of us are members of teams. People we love and care about count on each of us daily. Your level of discipline and follow though affects not only your life, but also the lives of everyone around you. When you know that your partner in work, marriage, and parenting has your back and that you have his or her back in return, you are feeling the strength of the cement that glues your relationship together. The more powerful your discipline muscle, the more consistently you can accomplish what needs to be done, and the more freedom your partner has to pursue your shared goals. If you are in a relationship where you have some issue with your partner's sense of discipline, start by looking at yourself. You'll be amazed at the way that discipline rubs off on others, especially those closest to you.

The challenge.

We are living in a sound bite world. We are constantly seeing images of instant food, instant relationships, and instant results, and we've come to expect that these are reasonable and attainable goals—they're not. The almost universal unease and frustration we are experiencing culturally is occurring because of this attitude. But anything that can please us instantly will just as quickly lose our interest. Substance is being replaced by flash, commitment by consumption, and precision by speed. We are losing our ability to create and appreciate lasting things of value. By the time you've reached my age (forty-eight), I'm sure you've felt the same dissatisfaction. I like the sense that something—or someone—has been the result of long-term effort and discipline. When I see a strong, healthy, beautiful twenty-someone, I don't even turn my head. When I see a strong, healthy, beautiful fifty-someone, I stop and stare. This is a person I can respect and admire. When I meet an enthusiastic, motivated, dreamer/creator fifty-someone, I know I've found a teacher. I recognize the face of discipline.

Follow this instinct to admire, respect, and value the results of discipline. Life is pure creation. Every thought, word, and deed drives us toward an outcome. All of civilization is built on long-term dedication to a goal; it's what makes us great and gives meaning to our lives. Your own discipline is the mindful act of consistently directing your personal power toward achieving the goals that are most meaningful to you.

WITH REGARD TO EXCELLENCE, IT IS NOT ENOUGH TO KNOW,
BUT WE MUST TRY TO HAVE AND USE IT.

ARISTOTLE

Growing Discipline

Performance experts in the fields of music, athletics, and business have come to agree that ten thousand hours is the gold standard for mastery, six thousand hours for professional excellence, and two thousand hours for functional proficiency. Broken down, an Olympic Gold medal looks like this: four hours a day of expert instruction and focused practice, five days a week, fifty weeks a year for ten years (4 x 5 x 50 x 10=10,000). This equation assumes a reasonable talent—far *less* then you might imagine—and a boatload of desire—far *more* than you might imagine. When you witness an extraordinary performance, it's a safe bet that the performer has paid for his gifts with that much discipline.

I realize that to most of us, the thought of ten thousand hours of anything is almost incomprehensible. However, the secret of peak performers is that they aren't working at all—they're playing. Wouldn't you love to play for ten thousand hours? Don't get me wrong: they are playing harder than most people ever work. The difference lies in their passion for what they do. I call this a "soul passion." Just as I believe that we have soul mates—men and women whose nature so resonates and complements our own that we are forever enriched by them—I believe that each of has soul passions, which take the form of careers, activities, and interests that give our creativity, talents, and joy wings. We have all met people we resonate with instantly, and who have been instruments in our lives for great joy and growth. When we connect with one of our soul passions, we get a similar feeling. Think of what it felt like when Rafael Nadal first touched a tennis racquet; when Bill Gates sat at a keyboard attached to a mainframe computer; when Beethoven first sat at a piano and created music; when Mother Theresa first touched a sick child's hand. In each of these moments, someone found a soul passion and came alive with purpose—now it's your turn.

Don't worry—your soul passion doesn't have to be anything huge. You are under no moral or global obligation to become the next Mother Teresa,

Bill Gates, or Ludwig van Beethoven. All you are looking for is an activity that feeds your soul. The bird watcher, the stamp collector, and the Civil War buff are all having their souls fed by playing at their passion. Passion is the elixir that transforms the drudgery associated with discipline into play.

FINDING YOUR SOUL PASSION.

As parents, we want to expose our children to as wide a variety of activities, cultures, and educational disciplines as possible. The reason for this is two-fold. First, we want our children to be as well rounded as possible, so that they can take advantage of as many opportunities as they can. Second, more importantly, we want them to find their soul passions!

If you weren't blessed with a childhood filled with adventures in learning—or even if you were—then start now. Take a class at your local community college, join a club that interests you, stretch your imagination, go to a yoga retreat, skydive, surf, climb a mountain, collect stamps, watch birds. I don't care what you do—just keep doing it until you find your way home. You'll know your home when you find one of your soul passions. It will fit you as well as your best friend does. Then get good at it, through steady, disciplined play.

By far, the happiest, healthiest, most productive, and engaging people I have ever met are those men and women who have discovered a way to play for a living. Steven Spielberg has loved the magic of movies his entire life, and Donald Trump has never stopped playing Monopoly. The architect who takes someone's dream and turns it into a home that person will love for generations, and the teacher who sees the love of learning come to life in a child's eye—all these people are playing at work. The more closely your profession is aligned with your passions, the happier and more successful you will be. If you love children and learning, get out from behind that cubicle and teach! Your passion might not always lead you to financial riches, but there is no one richer than the man or woman who is disciplined enough to create a way to spend life at a labor of love!

TAKING OUT THE TRASH.

I don't intend to create the illusion that a labor of love doesn't include plenty of unpleasant tasks. I'm sure there are plenty of things Spielberg hates about making movies, and Trump's game of Monopoly has taken him to bankruptcy court on more than one occasion. Peak performers understand that pursuing a dream costs you something in time and trouble, and they're glad to pay it. That's the final part of discipline—doing what needs to be done, even when it hurts.

I was recently running the stadium steps at Santa Barbara City College, and Olympic Volleyball Gold Medalists Todd Rogers and Phil Dalhausser were training there as well. Remember at the beginning of this section I mentioned being humbled by what others are doing with their blocks? Todd and Phil were jumping fours (feet together hopping over three steps at a time) all the way to the top of the stadium. As a trainer, I can assure you there are very few exercises as challenging or painful! As a success coach, I can also assure you that this level of discipline is the reason they won the Gold, and that the day I met up with them, they were right where they wanted to be, doing exactly what they wanted to be doing. Though they weren't playing the game they love in front of the fans they love, they were earning the right to do so! Be great! The world needs you!

I AM, INDEED, A KING, BECAUSE I KNOW HOW TO RULE MYSELF.

PIETRO ARETINO

Discipline Exercises

EXERCISE 1.

"Soul Passion" exploration is the key to discipline! What are two activities that bring you a great sense of joy, self-worth, and fulfillment? Teaching, learning, children, computers, art, music, nature—write down any two things that literally turn you on!

Two of my "Soul Passions" are _____ and

_____

EXERCISE 2.

On the left, write down two of your soul passions. Then, on the right, write your profession (and, yes, housewife/mother is a profession, and a noble one). Underneath, give yourself a score of 1 to 5—with 1 representing a perfect fit and 5 representing no connection whatsoever.

Soul Passion   Profession

1._____   _____

2._____

Alignment score:_____

EXERCISE 3.

Discipline means doing what needs to be done, when it needs to be done, regardless of what you want to do! Knowledge is not—and never will be—power, despite what some philosophers might tell you. Consistently applied (disciplined) knowledge is power! There is one action you need to take right now, and only you know what it is. Doing so will greatly improve the quality of your life. Indentify that action, and book it into your weekly calendar.

Answer the following question: what is one activity I have been putting off that I need to act on that will greatly improve the quality of my life? Examples include quitting smoking, starting a diet or exercise program, going back to school, mending a relationship.

Starting today, I will _____

_____

I have booked this activity into my daily planner: _____

Accomplished: _____

Be Strong!

Be strong!
We are not here to play, to dream, to drift;
We have hard work to do, and loads to lift;
Shun not the struggle—face it; 'tis God's gift.

Be strong!
Say not, "The days are evil. Who's to blame?"
And fold not the hands and acquiesce—Oh, shame!
Stand up, speak out, and bravely, in God's name.

Be strong!
It matters not how deep entrenched the wrong,
How hard the battle goes, the day how long;
Faint not—fight on! To-morrow comes the song.

MALTBIE D. BABCOCK

E
<u>ENTHUSIASM</u>

From Greek, entheos, meaning "in God." The creative, magnetic e-motion (energy in motion) that draws to us the people, resources, and events we need to achieve our goals.

ENTHUSIASM IS FED BY RESULTS AND THE POSITIVE, SUPPORTIVE PEOPLE WITH WHOM WE ALIGN OURSELVES.

GREAT TEACHERS DON'T just stuff our heads with information; they are catalysts for change. Good ones carry, nag, push, motivate, lead, beat, and sometimes even drag us to growth. However, every once in a while we meet truly great teachers who forever change who we are by simply being themselves.

It was 1983, and I was a junior at Cal Poly. Calling me a student would probably be a bit of a stretch. I had been placed on academic probation for missing most of my previous quarter's finals (a long story, mainly about a lack of enthusiasm), and I was struggling to stay awake and stay in school. It was seven o'clock, and I don't remember the class or the professor, but I remember what happened that morning. I was propped up in my chair leaning on my elbow, with a big cup of coffee, mentally preparing myself to slog through yet another hour and a half of whatever they were going to try to pour in my mostly vacant mind, when suddenly this man burst into the classroom as if from another world. He was a guest speaker, and he had the most engaging, contagious energy I had ever seen. He danced back and forth in front of our class, regaling us with poignant, funny, and amazing life stories. Through the sheer force of his personality, he pulled me forward in my chair. I was now wide awake, my pencil and feet tapping to the hypnotic beat of his voice. I remember looking around the room and realizing that this man had breathed life into a room full of college kids at an ungodly hour. A lightning bolt struck while he was describing the marathon he had just completed and the three women currently chasing him, one of whom he would take on his next adventure.

He had also just celebrated his ninetieth birthday. In a matter of minutes, this man had succeeded in destroying every myth I held about living and aging. He possessed more life, enthusiasm, and joy than many college students. My life's path was set that day, and my personal quest had become clear. I would discover the secret of ageless enthusiasm and one day do for others what this man had done for me.

Enthusiasm at Work

Our ability to achieve goals is directly proportional to the amount of enthusiasm we can develop and sustain during the creative process. Sustaining enthusiasm is linked directly to how closely our goals are aligned to our soul purpose. When you are turned on by an idea, you are moved into a highly magnetized and creative state. During these times of peak enthusiasm, you must open your awareness to any and all avenues to success. The pathway to success will often come disguised as a problem, failure, or breakdown, and by misreading the path, we lose the gift. Peak performers have developed the ability to take full advantage of these subtle opportunities.

Enthusiasm is created by the alignment of our actions to our soul purpose. Expecting to sustain high levels of enthusiasm through sheer discipline is one of the main reasons we fail to achieve goals.

Because enthusiasm is so important to the creative process, you need to nurture and protect it constantly. Focus on your long-term successes, not your temporary failures, and only share your goals with individuals you know to be supportive. Few things damage your enthusiasm and energy more than listening to someone give you all the reasons why your idea won't work—especially when this negative view is coming from someone you care about. We've discussed the reasons behind insulating yourself from negative people and negative energy in other sections, but this principle is especially important for the initial creative phase of any goal. Just as a pregnant mother nurtures her unborn child with nutrition, rest, and exercise, you should provide the same protective, nurturing environment for your goals—and your dreams. As an old friend of mine says, if someone on your team is rocking the boat, he had better be rowing it!

Intelligent, consistent action, driven by enthusiasm will draw to you everything needed to achieve the impossible.

EVERY GREAT AND COMMANDING MOMENT IN THE ANNALS OF THE WORLD IS THE TRIUMPH OF SOME ENTHUSIASM.

RALPH WALDO EMERSON

Growing Enthusiasm

We are born with certain genetic predispositions to skill sets and physical traits. Short – tall, left brain – right brain, analytical – creative, people person – loner. However, regardless of your predisposition and current skill level, as a creative being you have the ability to produce incredible growth in every area your life.

Enthusiasm is born and sustained as part of an energetic continuum. I know this statement sounds a little like wishful thinking, but bear with me. When we are engaged in an activity that feeds our soul (our soul passion), enthusiasm is a natural consequence. Enthusiasm directed toward an activity causes us to seek out specific knowledge related to it. Soul passion, enthusiasm, and knowledge drive us to take more action. These actions, which include study, training, and practice, lead us to results. When we achieve these results, they feed our souls and create more enthusiasm. This energetic continuum is an upward spiral of skill development, results, growth, and joy. Nothing else is as clear a path to success.

The more we feel the connection between our actions and our most important goals, the more consistent and effective we become. The young student with dreams of Harvard will have a much easier time doing homework than the young student with no ambition to go to college. The middle-aged man with dangerously high blood pressure will be much more consistent with his diet and exercise than the one with a big gut, but no serious health issues—none so far, anyway! Connection is everything. Seeing how today's actions are creating your goals and dreams are what keep you young, energetic, and enthusiastic.

The best way to grow and maintain high levels of enthusiasm is to structure your life in such a way that the largest percentage of your time is invested in soul-feeding activities. However, we will all face situations where we need to generate enthusiasm for an important task when we are feeling anything but enthusiastic. I recently lost both of my parents, and on the day of my father's funeral I had a new-client orientation. This is a vital part of my business, and this person had been referred to me by a very good friend. If we rescheduled, it would be weeks before we could connect again. By understanding how movement can control e-motions (energy in motion), I was able to honestly and enthusiastically share the benefits of my program by employing these powerful modeling techniques.

Modeling is not sustainable, but it is extremely effective in the short term. Science has discovered that our emotions drive our physiological responses. Happiness and feelings of well being cause us to smile. Excitement and enthusiasm bring about changes in our movement and speech patterns. Fear and anxiety cause our breathing to become quick and shallow and our heart rate and blood pressure to increase. Science has also discovered that by imitating a physical response our bodies work backwards and change our emotional state. By changing what you are doing with your body, you can actually change how you feel. As children, when we were bored and depressed our parents would tell us to go outside and play. What they were actually doing was changing our mood by changing our physiology. Smiling battles depression; consciously breathing more deeply and slowly eases fear and anxiety.

There are distinct speech and movement patterns associated with enthusiasm. By replicating the patterns we can re-create the emotion.

BAD HAIR DAYS.

As humans we will all have bad days. I can't tell you why, this just is. Maybe it's the moon, wave cycles, the planets, stars—why doesn't really matter. What matters is that we acknowledge them. Give yourself the freedom to take a day off, step away from the project, go play, go rest, lie on the couch, cry, read a book, or do nothing at all, but be loving and forgiving of yourself. Forcing yourself to be creative when you simply have no available juice will almost always backfire.

History is written by those men and women bold enough and powerful enough to do all of the things everyone believes to be impossible!

IT'S FAITH IN SOMETHING AND ENTHUSIASM FOR SOMETHING
THAT MAKES A LIFE WORTH LIVING.

OLIVER WENDELL HOLMES JR.

Enthusiasm Exercises

EXERCISE 1.

Think of the three most enthusiastic people you have known. These people may have been your teachers, partners, mentors, or friends, or had some other role in your life.

Write down their names here:

1._____

2._____

3._____

Now close your eyes and think of a time when you were actually swept away by the energy from one of these people. Describe that experience briefly here:

_____

_____

_____

_____

EXERCISE 2.

Relive the moment you just described and write down everything you can remember about that enthusiastic person's physical movement. List all the physiological actions you can recall. What did you hear in his or her voice? What were this person's body movements like? How fast or slow? How close was this person to you?

_____

_____

_____

_____

_____

_____

_____

_____

Now take all these memories and sensations and put them in a safe place in your memory. This whole set will tell you how to be enthusiastic and how to tell others about your enthusiasm. Be it. Live it. Show it.

EXERCISE 3.

Exercise your enthusiasm. Here's what to do with your enthusiasm—it's a lot of fun. You'll need to find a willing friend to participate in this exercise. Your objective is to sweep someone away with your enthusiasm about an activity you love. Communicate with this person in as much detail as possible about why this activity feeds your soul. Then have your friend accompany you and participate in the activity with you. You might read aloud your favorite book, cook your favorite meal, join in a yoga class, climb a mountain, or go surfing; you might take your companion to a museum or to your company. Whatever you choose, share your joy simply, deeply, and honestly. After he or she has participated in your joy, flip roles. Allow your friend to share a joyful activity or place with you. Have as much fun as possible, be as open and honest as possible, and play!

Look To This Day

Listen to the Exhortation of the Dawn!
Look to this Day!
For it is Life, the very Life of Life.
In its brief course lie all the
Verities and Realities of your Existence.
The Bliss of Growth,
The Glory of Action,
The Splendor of Beauty;
For Yesterday is but a Dream,
And To-morrow is only a Vision;
But To-day well lived makes
Every Yesterday a Dream of Happiness,
And every Tomorrow a Vision of Hope.
Look well therefore to this Day!
Such is the Salutation of the Dawn!

KALIDASA

F
<u>FOCUS</u>

The ability to harness and direct all of your physical, mental, and emotional energies to the task at hand.

Lao Tzu said, the journey of a thousand miles begins with one step; I add to that, Focus on putting all your energy into making every step great.

AT THIS POINT in our training, it's important to remember that I view each of these twenty-six keys as a learnable skill set. I want you to practice and master them the same way a basketball player or a golfer practices and masters the skills he needs to improve his game. Your goal is not just to read each chapter; your goal is to develop, employ, and own each key principle.

Focus at Work

The mixture of blood, sweat, and old canvas has a scent that stays with you, especially when the blood and sweat are your own. The canvas felt remarkably cool, and I remember not being in any hurry to get up. I thought about springing back up on my feet, then thought, "Aaahhh, not really." I'm pretty sure I crawled over to the ropes and pulled myself up, slowly and painfully. It was hard to see because blood from the split in my forehead had run into both of my eyes. My opponent had landed a beautiful elbow strike and slammed my brain into the back of my skull. Apparently I wasn't as good a fighter as I had thought moments earlier. As a brand new first-degree black belt, I had gone to Benny "the Jet's" kickboxing studio in Van Nuys to spread my wings and test my skills. I was partnered with a kickboxer with only six months experience, and I was convinced that my three years of martial arts training would be more than enough to carry the day. Instead of winning the match, I learned an important lesson: self-esteem that isn't backed up by competence can be hazardous to your ego—and your health.

This lesson, or as I like to call it, this "attitude adjustment session," motivated me to spend the next five years seeking out the best fighters and instructors in the United States. Luck, chance, and a great deal of hard work brought me to a seminar taught by Stephen K. Hayes, a master instructor, author, and Black Belt Hall of Fame member. Amazed at the simplicity, honesty, and effectiveness of his approach, I knew I had found my teacher, but there was one problem: Mr. Hayes was no longer accepting any new individual students. Instead of becoming discouraged, I purchased all of his books and training manuals, got copies of publications featuring his techniques, and began traveling all over the country attending his seminars. I spent all my free time reading these materials from cover to cover. I did this week after week, month after month, intent on squeezing out one more piece of information, one more insight.

My total focus on training with Stephen Hayes served me well, and within a year, I had my first private lesson in his Ohio home. Two years later, we were partners and together founded the Stephen K. Hayes Quest Centers, where today To-Shin Do is being taught to students all over the United States.

Ultimately, what I learned from these three years of training was simple: when all of your energy is directed towards a specific goal, you will succeed.

How do you direct your energy effectively? This illustration might help you understand the answer more clearly. Imagine two powerful generators—one connected to an ordinary light bulb, the other to a laser—with both receiving the same amount of energy. While the light bulb's radiance is dispersed and lost within yards of its source, the laser beam can go on for miles. The key to this difference in effectiveness is focus. The reason so few people fulfill their potential has little to do with their personal power and everything to do with their ability to direct it in a focused manner. We don't need more hours in the day; we need to be more focused during the hours we have.

Many real-life situations show the truth of this idea. For instance, fitness industry data reveals that fewer than 10 percent of gym members train consistently. Of the 10 percent who do train, most are wasting their time with inefficient, ineffective workouts. As a sports fitness specialist for over a decade, I have witnessed countless one-hour workouts degenerate into fifteen minutes of training, blended with forty-five minutes of chat sessions, resting, flirting, going to the water station, or visiting the bathroom. Even consistent work will produce little or no result if it is unfocused. When you meet someone who regularly goes to the gym, but still looks weak or flabby, you've met a fitness light bulb.

However, when you see a body you admire, odds are you are looking at a diet and exercise laser beam. If you want to chat, go to Starbucks; if you want to train, then train. When I am working with a physique transformation client, I have one simple rule: if your mouth is moving, so is your body. Focused individuals avoid time stealers at all cost, and nothing steals time from you like aimless chatter.

Time theft happens at work, too. Corporate performance data suggest that the average employee produces approximately four hours of results for every eight hours worked. Again, at least half of our lifetime is wasted chatting, web surfing, shopping, reading and writing e-mail, and catching up at the coffee station. Wouldn't it be far better to spend five hours on focused production and find yourself working 20 percent more effectively than your competition? Then you could redirect your energy to career advancement, continued education, and marketing yourself and your company. Focused team members create their own job security. Peak performers are the laser beams of the universe, consistently directing their energies to the task at hand, completing it and redirecting their focus toward the next event.

YOU CAN'T DEPEND ON YOUR EYES WHEN YOUR
IMAGINATION IS OUT OF FOCUS.

MARK TWAIN

Growing Focus

Do you remember playing dodge ball as a child? These days, many people think the game is a little too brutal, but I still find that it has a lot of value as a great focus-growing exercise. It has what I call "the truth of the blade"; it's an activity that demands focus because the consequence of distraction is much greater than usual. In knife fighting, for example, you absolutely must focus, or you will pay a painful price. Knife fighters train with semi-sharp wood or dulled steel blades; both will break skin and ribs if your timing is wrong. When countering a full speed attack, you must be a laser beam. It only takes one or two excruciating mistakes to bring you back on task. Thoughts of children, spouses, bills, worries about the economy all disappear. To develop the level of focus necessary for high-level knife fighting, we use a consequence progression—and hundreds of hours of training. We begin teaching combat focus with slow-speed, choreographed movements using only our empty hands. As the students' skills improve, they learn how to read different types of attacks from different angles, and we increase the speed and complexity of the attacks. The goal is to bring a student's combat skills and focus to a level that will allow us to use free-form, full-speed attacks with weapons—exactly as a merciless enemy would in real combat. These drills are forced, moving meditations and a very advanced form of training. While this is an extreme example of growing focus, you can imagine how effective it is. In Buddhist traditions, this level of focus is known as "No Mind," whereas in the West, we call it the "zone" or "void."

Sports, education, and business are dominated by individuals who have the ability to consistently touch the "zone." This occurs when the veil of separation is removed from the participant and the activity. You become the movement, the swing, the dance, the piece of art. It is one of the most beautiful of all human experiences, occurring when you have a complete connection to each moment and your surroundings.

They say we can get lost in an event, a movie, a book, our lovers eyes, or in nature. I couldn't disagree more; I believe it is in these moments of pure focus that we find ourselves. When you are at work, work; when you are at play, play; when you are with your family, love. The more frequently we touch the zone, the easier it is to find it again.

As Willie Mays once said, "It isn't hard to be good from time to time in sports. What's tough is being good every day." To be that consistent, you need to develop the highest degree of skill possible. To do that, you need to create a progressive series of challenges to match your growing proficiency. This truth applies to all physical, mental, and emotional skill-set development. This progressive series of challenges is also known as negative stimulation, which we have covered in length in previous sections. As with attitude, a supportive environment is vital to the development of our focus muscle. The gardener builds raised beds, mixes nutrients in the soil, and installs watering systems and fences; all these environmental factors are designed to give fruits, flowers, and vegetables the best chance of growth. We need to ensure that our work and play environments help us grow. Your creative space should be free of clutter, and you should be able to insulate yourself from as many distractions as possible. Close your door, turn off your phone, turn the radio off or down, shut off your e-mail, and then create. The more easily distracted a person is, the more protected the creative space needs to be. Home offices and the Internet tend to be less than ideal for a person with a weak focus muscle.

We all have the ability to focus. I spent years training children with ADD and ADHD, and I learned two things: first, these children tend to be extremely intelligent; and second, when they are engaged in an activity they find engaging, they are laser beams. Try pulling a child diagnosed with ADD away from a favorite video game or pulling Michael Phelps out of the water, and you'll know what I mean.

As we proceed through our weekly diet of performance tips, you will discover many overlapping principles. For instance, it is much easier to keep your focus while engaged in a soul passion than in an activity you don't enjoy.

CONCENTRATE ALL YOUR THOUGHTS UPON THE WORK AT HAND. THE SUN'S RAYS DO NOT BURN UNTIL BROUGHT TO A FOCUS.

ALEXANDER GRAHAM BELL

Focus Exercises

EXERCISE 1.

Prepare your creative space. While sitting at your desk or work station, look around and mentally place a +, –, or 0 next to each item. (This is similar to the exercise we did in the attitude section.) The + items add to your productivity, the – items detract from it, and the 0 items have no impact. Immediately get rid of all – items and as many 0 items you can. The goal is to create an uncluttered, motivating workspace.

All week, be mindful of the time stealers and list those that are interfering with your productivity. By simply identifying them, you will begin to guard yourself against them.

EXERCISE 2.

This exercise introduces you to a basic meditation. It should take anywhere between five and twenty minutes. Find a quiet, uncluttered, beautiful space, either indoors or outdoors—it doesn't matter. Sit on a towel, pillow, or chair—again, it doesn't matter. If you know how to assume a full or half-lotus position, do so; if not, sit and cross your legs. If you are in a chair, sit with your feet on the ground hip-width apart, making sure your back doesn't touch the chair. Your spine and breath are the most important physical components of this exercise. Imagine a cable attached to the top of your head and lifting you toward the sky, lengthening your spine. Your breathing is deep, through the diaphragm. With every inhale, your stomach extends, and with every complete exhale, your shoulders relax around your tall, long spine. Take ten deep, slow, centering breaths, counting down from ten to one; repeat the phrases listed below with each inhale and exhale. Stay with the phrase for as long as it resonates with you. When you begin to lose focus, move on to the next phrase.

- I inhale and am aware of my body; I exhale and am aware of my body.
- I inhale and experience peace; I exhale and experience peace.
- I inhale and know gratitude; I exhale and know gratitude.

As different thoughts pop into your mind, let them go, and return to the exercise without judgment. The goal is to learn to quiet and direct your mind. The ability to focus on only one thought for a minute is considered a high-level skill. Play with the exercise, and enjoy these mental push-ups. When your mind no longer cooperates, slowly open your eyes, then stretch your shoulders and spine. You have completed the exercise.

Before any creative project, do this basic meditation, return to your protected workspace, and see how much better your focus and productivity become!

EXERCISE 3.

Write down the previous five performance ABCs and one key component of each. If you can't recall these, go back and review. Remember, success is a never-ending process. Never stop training; never stop learning; never stop growing! History is written by those men and women bold enough and powerful enough to do all of the things everyone believes to be impossible! Be great! The world needs you!

Invictus

Out of the night that covers me,
Black as the Pit from pole to pole,
I thank whatever gods may be
For my unconquerable soul.

In the fell clutch of circumstance
I have not winced nor cried aloud.
Under the bludgeonings of chance
My head is bloody, but unbowed.

Beyond this place of wrath and tears
Looms but the Horror of the shade,
And yet the menace of the years
Finds, and shall find, me unafraid.

It matters not how strait the gate,
How charged with punishments the scroll,
I am the master of my fate:
I am the captain of my soul.

WILLIAM EARNEST HENLEY

G
<u>GOALS</u>

1. Anything you are committed to being, doing, or having. 2. The act of creating your life in advance.

PEAK PERFORMERS RECOGNIZE THAT JOY IS FOUND
AS MUCH IN SETTING YOUR GOALS AS IN ACHIEVING THEM.

I WAS RUNNING the stadium steps at Santa Barbara City College about a year ago when I suddenly had an insight into setting and achieving goals. There's nothing particularly remarkable about running up those stadium steps—hundreds of people do it every week. I run them a lot too, but what made this day different was the argument I had with myself on the way. I had spent the past three nights sleeping on the couch because my wife and the two girls had been sick with a bad stomach flu. I had been taking care of them while trying to avoid getting sick myself, which isn't easy to do when you live in a 900-square-foot yurt. (In case you don't know, a yurt is a house-sized tent commonly used in Mongolia. The reason I live in one in California is a story for another time.) I had some excellent arguments against running the stadium steps. For one, I hadn't had a good night's sleep in three days; running those steps might overtax my immune system and give us a full house of vomiting invalids. I had to get home and start working on this week's performance tips, too. Besides, I'm sure the girls still needed me well enough to help them, and there weren't going to be any parking spots, and running stadiums sucks, and I'm already a little nauseous, and stadiums always make me feel sick … and so on. The arguments and whining continued in my head, right up until I parked and got out of the car. As usual, I started feeling better as soon as I started moving. I actually ended up with a faster run time than I had thought possible, but even so, when I sprinted the last flight of steps, a wave of nausea hit me, and I asked myself why, why, why? Then, in one of those brilliant moments of clarity, I knew: I ran because I had a great dad.

In 2009, he passed away at the age of eighty-seven. On Father's Day that year, my dad, my brother, my daughter, and I went on a two-hour horseback ride. Honestly, who gets to do that with a father in his eighties? I was lucky enough to have forty-six years with a dad who could do almost anything with his children and grandchildren. We rode horses and hunted together; we fixed pipes, fences, and anything else that didn't work. In his seventies and eighties, he played soccer, sailed, drove tractors, and rode horses with his grandchildren. He even did a head stand on his seventy-fifth birthday after a few too many glasses of wine, which was probably my fault, or at least the wine part was. On his eighty-fifth birthday, our entire family was invited to a breakfast ride at the Alisal Guest Ranch, a spectacularly beautiful resort here in the Santa Ynez Valley. My dad was treated like the guest of honor, and I could see how much the cowboys respected him. They knew he had spent his life on horses, and that day he looked like the star of an old western. He sat tall and comfortable in the saddle, proud to be there and even more proud of his family. I can still see my dad and the rest of my family on horseback, loping back from breakfast across a meadow. My daughter yelled out, "I have the coolest grandfather in the world!" She was right, but he didn't just wake up one day and find that he had magically become cool. His coolness was the result of a lifetime of setting big, bold goals and meeting them. He included fitness, longevity, and time with his family in those goals—and achieved them, one after the other, every day of his long life.

That's the reason I ran the stadiums that day, and the reason I've run them on many days since then. I intend to be every bit the father and grandfather my dad was to my kids. They deserve nothing less!

Goals at Work

Have you ever heard the basic questions of journalism: who, what, when, where, how, and why? They're the key components that must go in every story, and usually, they're the first thing that everybody learns about storytelling. What most people forget is that the most important story we will ever write is our own, and you only get to be the hero if you write the story that way. The doctor fighting aids in Africa, the rodeo cowboy strapped to the back of a bull, the Broadway actress singing her soul out on stage, the commodities broker trading millions in the blink of an eye, and the fireman who charges into a burning building all have something in common: they wrote the story of their lives with the same who, what, when, where, how, and why questions.

Here are the three most important things you can do to write your own story the way you want it:

1. *Work on you.* Develop a plan, and every week dedicate time to strengthening your body, mind, and spirit.
2. *Set goals.* Write, edit, and review these goals consistently. Rewrite your life's vision and plan as you go, but don't stop setting those goals.
3. *Live it today.* Just go out and do it! Don't wait for a perfect plan or a perfect moment; it will never happen. Do it now! Do it now! Do it now! The game ends the same for all of us. It's what we do with the days we have the makes a difference.

Goal setting is one of the most creative, empowering, and enjoyable exercises you will ever do. You literally get to tell the story of your life in advance. Whether you're the hero or the victim, in the lead or in a supporting role, the casting, the stage, and the players are all up to you. Even better, you have the power to change the story any time you want, although you'd be surprised how rarely people rewrite the script. Remember, it will never turn out exactly as planned because like any good story, it will grow and change as the author grows and changes. The universe has a way of making its own changes too, and that's why you need to get going on this now.

Starting soon is important. Make sure you take the time to write it yourself *right now*, because if you don't, the universe will do it for you. That version of your life might turn out OK, but it will never feel like the story you really wanted. I knew a boy who wanted to date, but he thought he needed a car to do that. He got a job in order to get a car, so that he could go on a date, like millions of boys across America and around the world. Before he really had a chance to learn about love and life, his girlfriend got pregnant. Then he had a car, a wife, and a baby, so he had to get a house and a different job to pay for the house and the car and to feed the baby and his wife. He worked at the job for forty years, and then he died. His life story isn't the saddest story you've ever read, but it isn't any different from a lot of others either. The rich, fulfilling life he wanted, full of goals and dreams and achievements—along with the car, the wife, the baby, and the house—never quite happened. You see, he hadn't written a life story with those things that would have made it interesting and would have made him feel as if he truly owned what he had. That's a shame because his wife and baby deserved to be part of the rich, fulfilling life he never had and to share their own rich, fulfilling lives with someone who truly appreciated the joys of family life. Remember, this sad story isn't about how having a family keeps you from living out your dreams—it's about how failing to live out your dreams keeps you from appreciating everything, including your family.

The key to goal setting, or writing the story of you, is to think big, be bold, and write it as though you really were a child of God and deserving of all the love, abundance, adventures, and friendships you can handle. Remember, people who have much less than you, have created much more. And it doesn't matter how old you think you are, older people are starting, pursuing, and achieving bigger goals every day. Fifty is a great age to go back to college. Sixty is perfect for learning how to rock climb. And seventy-year-old surfers rule. Did I mention the ninety-year-old marathon runner? Your best days lie before you! Go out there and live them!

Here are the big questions: Who do you intend to be? What skills, knowledge, passions, and strengths are you committed to possessing? When, and in what order are you going to achieve these goals, allowing them to open up even more possibilities in your life? Where would you love to go to learn, study, train, and live? How will you get access to the people, places, and events you need to experience the greatest joy, power, love, abundance, and contribution in your life? Why? Why? Why? Why are you doing any of it? Why will achieving any of these goals bring you more joy, health, love, friendship, abundance, and understanding? Attack every goal with the question why? And make sure the answer resonates deeply and clearly in your soul! If your why is big enough, you can accomplish anything. If you can't justify the why, then drop the goal.

WHATEVER THE MIND CAN CONCEIVE AND BELIEVE, IT WILL ACHIEVE!

NAPOLEON HILL

Growing Goals

Right now, I'm going to tell you how it all works. It's a little philosophical, but stay with me—it'll be worth it. Everything in our future—the person we may become, all we may do, and everything we may have—exists already, right now, in the our thoughts as potential energy. How we focus our intellect, our emotion, and our actions determines whether we attract or repel thoughts.

If you look around you right now, you can see that everything around you began as someone's thought energy. The coffeemaker you used for this morning's brew, the computer in your office, even the chair you are sitting on—all of these things began as someone's idea. Thoughts are things; they can harm and heal; they can create and destroy. Thoughts are often more challenging than physical things. I've had a broken arm (a physical injury), and I've had a broken heart (a thought injury); I'll take a broken arm over a broken heart any day. Think about the impact your thought patterns have on your body: stress, a condition manifested by what and how we think, can cause cancer, ulcers, high cholesterol, high blood pressure, heart attacks, and strokes.

The older we are, the more the physical elements in our life represent our most consistent thought patterns. Goal setting is the conscious act of directing and controlling as many of the variables that make up your life experience as possible and acting consistently with these goals when the universe throws unforeseen events in your path. Highly successful men and women will tell you that unexpected adverse events—a perceived failure, the death of a loved one, the loss of a job—ultimately led them to many of their greatest successes. The only variables that you have direct control over are your thoughts, words, and deeds. The more clearly you have defined yourself and the more consistently you have lived by these self-defined roles, the more successfully you will respond to each of life's challenges.

Very few people exercise the discipline needed to control their thoughts, words, and deeds. How many times have you wasted your energy on negative thought patterns or destructive behaviors? We all need powerful, motivating goals because they are what direct our thoughts, words, and deeds. Living mindfully means that you are paying attention to, and directing your power toward, the things in life that matter the most to you.

If you have never done a goal-setting session, then your first one is going to require some intellectual sweat and a few hours, but I promise you they will be some of the best hours you'll ever spend in terms of return on your time.

SETTING GOALS.

The best way to set goals is to make sure they are SMART, which stands for:

SPECIFIC. If you want to set a fitness goal, use terms that relate concretely to your body, as in, "I want to weigh 165 pounds and have a body fat percentage of 8 percent," instead of, "I want to look good." Say to yourself, "I want live in a 2,500-square foot, sustainably built, ranch-style home on five acres in a beautiful valley in California," instead of, "I want a nice house."

MEASURABLE. Body fat can be measured, pretty can't. Fifteen thousand dollars a month can be measured, financial security can't.

ACHIEVABLE. Has this goal been accomplished before? Do you currently have the resources necessary for achieving it? What's possible may change over time; but begin realistically. As your ability increases, so will the scope of what's achievable, and you can always set your sights higher as you go. If you have never run a four-minute mile, it probably isn't an achievable goal. Decide to run a twelve-minute mile, and then try for an eleven-and-a-half-minute mile. Keep competing with yourself, and who knows where it will take you!

RELEVANT. Ask yourself the big why question. Why is it essential that you achieve this goal? What will it cost you if you don't? Will achieving it bring you health, friendship, opportunity, love, joy, or abundance? Will failure lead to their loss? What will it bring you? What motivates you to do it?

TIME SET. Goals are dreams with a deadline. Time lines force us to take action and are how we quantify our progress. If your goal is to lose five pounds in twenty-eight days, then you need to lose a pound and a quarter per week. If you fall short of your first week's goal, then you know what you are doing isn't working. That situation leaves you with two possibilities: (1) you either need a better plan or (2) you need to implement the plan you have more effectively. Either way, setting a time by which your goals must be accomplished will make you face up to the difficulties you are having and deal with them.

> WHEN IT IS OBVIOUS THAT THE GOALS CANNOT BE REACHED,
> DON'T ADJUST THE GOALS, ADJUST THE ACTION STEPS.
>
> CONFUCIUS

Goals Exercises

EXERCISE 1.

This nine-step exercise, Writing the Story of You, requires one to two hours of uninterrupted time. You need to be totally insulated, no calls, no kids, no e-mails, so find a quiet place where you can be creative. You will need a clock and something to record your story: a computer, a dictation machine, or pen and paper, whatever you find easiest to use. Then take the following steps:

STEP 1: HAVE A BASIC MEDITATION.

This step is basically the same meditation that you encountered in the chapter on focus, but this time, you'll be using it to begin setting your goals.

Just as you did then, find a quiet, uncluttered, beautiful space, either indoors or outdoors, and sit on a towel, pillow, or chair. Assume a full or half-lotus position, if you can; if not, sit and cross your legs. Imagine a cable attached to the top of your head and lifting you toward the sky, lengthening your spine. Your breathing is deep, through the diaphragm. With every inhale, your stomach extends, and with every complete exhale, your shoulders relax around your tall, long spine. Take ten deep, slow, centering breaths, counting down from ten to one; then, repeat the phrases listed below with each inhale and exhale. Stay with the phrase for as long as it resonates with you; when you begin to lose focus, move on to the next one.

+ I inhale and am aware of my body; I exhale and am aware of my body.
+ I inhale and experience peace; I exhale and experience peace.
+ I inhale and know gratitude; I exhale and know gratitude.

As different thoughts pop into your mind, let them go and return to the exercise without judgment. Quiet and direct your mind for a minute or so at a time. When you finish, slowly open your eyes, then stretch your shoulders and spine.

STEP 2: ACKNOWLEDGE YOUR CREATIVE POWER.

Take a moment to reflect upon and be grateful for your creative gifts. Be clear on the significance of what you are about to do. You are taking responsibility for the creation of your future. You are not a victim or a pawn in someone else's story; you are the master of your fate, you are the captain of your soul!

74

STEP 3: CREATE YOUR TEN-YEAR VISUALIZATION.

Imagine what you will see ten years into your future, and start writing. Use the present tense and as much detail as you can. It doesn't have to be perfect; remember, this is a life-long work in progress. Check your clock and write as much as you can in fifteen minutes. Here's mine, for example:

> My name is Bill Poett. I am fifty-seven years old. I weigh 165 pounds, and my body fat is 8 percent. I have been happily married to the love of my life, Robin, for thirteen years. We have three daughters: Miranda, 27; Kayla, 17; and Becca, 11. We live in a beautiful, off-grid 2,500-square foot, sustainably built home on Rancho San Julian surrounded by beautiful, drought-resistant landscaping, a vineyard, and horses ...

Include every aspect of your life in as much detail as possible:

+ Education
+ Career
+ Hobbies and interests
+ Adventures and travel
+ Service to others
+ Anything else that is important to you

STEP 4: MAKE A FIVE-YEAR PLAN.

Move five years into the future, and connect the previous story with this one, working backward from the ten-year vision. Take ten minutes for this step.

STEP 5: MAKE A ONE-YEAR PLAN.

Move one year into the future, and visualize what you need to do to get where you want to be for your ten-year vision, again working backward. Now is the time to get into the details, including what skills you have developed and what changes have taken place in your life to move you on the right path. Take ten minutes for this step.

STEP 6: MAKE A SIX-MONTH PLAN.

Move six months into the future, and work backward from your ten-year vision to that point in your life. This time, become even more detailed, listing what skills you already have, which ones you are developing, and what changes you are implementing to get on the right path. Devote five minutes to this step.

STEP 7: REVISE YOUR GOALS.

Go back and attack each goal. Make sure they are truly important to you and the life you are committed to creating. Make any rewrites and changes that feel appropriate.

STEP 8: PUT YOUR GOALS ON YOUR CALENDAR.

Now that you have a clear vision for your future, enter in your day planner the top three action steps you are committed to accomplishing this week that will best move you toward your six-month goals and objectives.

STEP 9: STAY ON COURSE.

Review your goals at least three times per week, the more you can pour yourself into them emotionally and see them as already existing, the more effective they will be. Once a week, dedicate time to revisit, reflect, and rewrite them.

Count That Day Lost

If you sit down at set of sun And count the acts that you have done,
And, counting, find One self-denying deed, one word
That eased the heart of him who heard,
One glance most kind That fell like sunshine where it went—
Then you may count that day well spent.

But if, through all the livelong day,
You've cheered no heart, by yea or nay—
If, through it all You've nothing done that you can trace

That brought the sunshine to one face—
No act most small That helped some soul and nothing cost—
Then count that day as worse than lost.

GEORGE ELIOT

H
<u>HEROISM</u>

Taking appropriate action in the face of fear or danger.

I THINK THEY GOT IT WRONG IN THE SIXTIES. LIFE ISN'T ABOUT FINDING
YOURSELF; LIFE IS ABOUT MINDFULLY CREATING YOUR HERO SELF
BY YOUR EVERY THOUGHT, WORD, AND DEED.

IN 1994, MY martial arts academy was named a top one hundred school out of the fifteen thousand operating in the United States. While we were teaching a very practical and effective form of self-defense, the key to our success was that we were using combat techniques to teach personal growth and development. Many of the performance ABCs that I am sharing with you today were first tested and implemented at the academy.

One afternoon, a hopeful, worried, single mother of a five-year-old boy came into our school. Her son's teacher had recommended the program as a way to help him build much-needed confidence. He was one of the most painfully shy children I had ever met. They walked into the introductory room, and he looked as if he were actually glued to his mother's hip. I quickly discovered that he wasn't just shy—he had absolutely no physical coordination. As I took him through some basic movements, he tripped over his foot, and before he hit the mat, his mom flew out of her chair and actually caught him. I'd never seen anyone move that fast. As a life coach, this was one of the most heart-wrenching scenes I had ever witnessed. Of all the challenges and obstacles this boy would face on his path to becoming a powerful, independent human, one of the greatest would be his own mother. Driven by her instinct to protect her son, this loving woman was acting in a way that would cripple him. After our session, I had a long talk with the mother. I asked if she had the courage to let her boy stumble, fall, get hurt, and get back up again. Could she suppress her instincts and allow him to grow into the man she wished him to be? She said she could, and four years later he stood before me at a black belt graduation grinning. Tears streamed down both our faces while his mother watched—from a distance.

Sometimes heroes are even closer to home. My daughter lost her mother, Whendy, to liver failure during my daughter's freshman year of high school. She had fought for her life against the disease for a year—and lost. We were devastated. One of Whendy's last wishes was to rest on the ranch near her daughter's home. My dad, my brother, and I had built a bench on the particular spot she wanted, a beautiful grass-covered slope that overlooks the valley where we often go riding and near where my sister, Susan, also rests in eternal peace. When we had a small celebration of Whendy's life there with her family and friends, my daughter, clear eyed and with a voice as pure and beautiful as any I have ever heard, sang a final song for her mother, "Wishing You Were Somehow Here Again." Whendy had always loved to hear Miranda sing, and we were sure Whendy was listening from wherever she was. As the depth of Miranda's love and pain over her loss resonated through every breath, I prayed, "God, when I lose my parents, help me show the same level of love, grace, and courage that my daughter is showing right now."

It is not our job to protect our children from the world; we can't. Rather, it is our job to do everything in our power to help prepare them for it.

Heroes at Work

Real heroes usually look nothing like the ones we see in the movies. During my ten years as a close-quarter combat instructor, I had the opportunity to work and train with many of our nation's most elite warriors. One of the most surprising things I noticed was that the more capable these warriors were, the less their outward appearance seemed to show it. In almost every case, those who had the most lethal skills were the most quiet, benign, and respectful people. True confidence never feels the need to assert itself, and confidence comes from having real ability. When we imagine heroes, we tend to think of firefighters rushing into burning buildings or soldiers fighting to save their comrades—and those are heroes, true enough. While these acts require tremendous courage, they are often performed as a reflex to an extreme event; very little conscious thought takes place in an emergency. The people involved simply act and respond according to their training, and we appreciate their heroism, to be sure. But there's another kind of courage too. All too often, the everyday heroes in our lives go unnoticed. The single mother who works two jobs to get her child through college; the father with cancer who goes on fighting through tremendous pain, so he can stay with his family a little longer; the school teacher who pours herself into every class, every day, in a failing school system—these are all heroes. True heroism is consistent action taken without regard for medals, accolades, or thanks, because the job needs to be done.

A HERO DRAWS INSPIRATION FROM THE VIRTUE OF HIS ANCESTORS.

JOHANN WOLFGANG VON GOETHE

Growing Your Inner Hero

Are you a hero, a victim, or something between the two? As you write the story of your life, you will have to determine where and what you stand for, so the decision to be a hero is yours to make. The challenge you face, as you begin to define yourself in the world, is that the moment you stand for something, by definition, you are standing against something, and this will take courage. As a hero, you take responsibility for your life and the lives of those around you. As a victim, your life, your joy, and success are at the mercy and will of others.

How do you overcome fear? Warriors for millennia have overcome their fears with a simple technique: embrace the very thing that threatens you. Once you have faced what you fear at close range, you will discover that you have destroyed fear itself, the most dangerous of enemies. When you are physically, mentally, and emotionally prepared to handle the worst the world has to offer, you are free to direct all of your energies into achieving your goals. A great teacher of mine once said that he would do anything to avoid a fight, but if he had to fight, he was good with God, and his life insurance was paid up. The person with nothing to fear is the last person you ever want to meet in combat. The value of using combat techniques to teach life principles is that the consequences of failure are so dire, they make everything else pale by comparison. Many of the men who survived the assault on the beaches of Normandy went on to become great civic and business leaders after the war. Think about it: what else during the rest of their lives would ever scare them?

What scares you? Is it having a job interview, asking your dream someone on a date, speaking in front of a big crowd, asking the boss for a raise, being rejected, getting injured? Fear weakens you; conquering it empowers you and frees your energies for the task at hand. Start by realizing that your fears are really False Evidence Appearing Real—FEAR. In other words, you can cut fear down to size by understanding how little you really have to be afraid of—most of what scares you is in your mind. Then practice "Worst Case Embrace," a technique mastered by the Japanese Samurai, some of the greatest warriors of all time. To achieve the state of fearlessness necessary for them to fight with almost limitless skill and courage, they learned to accept the possibility of death as a noble ally to their ultimate goal: victory. By embracing the possibility of dying in battle, they removed their fear of it. Once free of fear, they were then free to win, and they won, over and over, against overwhelming odds.

The Samurai showed the most extreme form of Worst Case Embrace, but the technique, proven in battle, can be modified to fit any of the much lesser fears we face today. As a professional speaker, I used Worst Case Embrace to be as effective in front of large audiences as I was in one-on-one situations. I did this by imagining the worst outcome possible—to a ridiculous extent. I pictured a huge audience, all there to hear the most significant presentation of my life. I saw myself walking on stage, looking at the thousands of eyes staring at me, and then wetting myself. Then I would be so distraught that I would throw up on myself and pass out.

A pretty horrifying scenario, isn't it? In my imagination, I saw what would happen even after the worst speaking disaster I could dream up. Some nice people would carry me off-stage, wake me up, and clean me off, and then I would do a life-check—a quick inventory of where I stand with regard to the things that really matter. I would discover that I hadn't gone blind or developed cancer, my children hadn't been sold into slavery, my wife still loved me, and basically, everything was still OK. Even if the worst I could imagine happened, I would survive. Once I knew that I could survive the worst that situation could throw at me, I was able to focus all of my energies on a great presentation.

When I was a martial arts trainer, I used the Worst Case Embrace visualization as one of the final exercises for my black belt candidates. We began with a basic centering meditation, and then I had them imagine being tested in front of all of their peers, instructors, and friends. At the conclusion of the test, they would we be informed that they had not passed and would have to wait three months for a retest. We conducted the visualization in great detail so they could feel the actual pain of failure. When we finished the meditation, I would ask each candidate a simple question: If you actually failed your black belt test, what would you do—quit or train harder and come back an even stronger candidate? If they said "quit," then we knew they weren't ready, but if the answer was "come back even stronger," then we knew they were.

Worst Case Embrace is important, because it prepares you for anything, including the worst thing you can imagine, which sometimes actually happens. Almost everyone has heard of Chuck Norris, but few people know that he actually faced what my students feared most—he failed his first black belt test. The pain of this experience drove him to come back, pass the test, and go on to become one of the most successful martial artists in history. Once you have learned to manage fear and have dedicated yourself to a weekly diet of body, mind, and spirit training, the world will open her doors to you.

Here are some tips on being a hero:

- Be powerful by taking responsibility. The more of your life, relationships, and the world you take responsibility for, the more powerful you become.
- Don't wait for someone else to make it better. Remember, if it's to be, it's up to me!
- Don't worry about mistakes. Being a hero doesn't mean being perfect. The bigger the vision, the more frequently you will fail and screw up. When you do, own it, apologize for it, learn from it, and then forgive yourself and move on.
- Choose to be a hero. It really is a choice, so choose to do heroic things in both large and small arenas. The key is to create the habit of heroic action, so that the choices get easier, even when the stakes are high.

- Remember, even those small acts of heroism add up. Pick up one piece of trash every day; make one person smile; open a door for someone.
- Learn some history. Being a hero can and does have huge consequences. Reading about people who have changed the world in a positive way through heroic action can inspire you to do the same.

YOU ARE A HERO.

Sometimes you have to learn who you aren't in order to become who you really want to be. Because I grew up in a wonderful family with two great parents, it took me a long time to learn an important lesson: sometimes life sucks. Forgive me if I'm offending everybody who finds something good in every problem, but some things are awful. You can't tell a woman who was raped, a teenager who lost a parent, or a father raising two small children alone after their mother has been killed by a drunk driver that there is something good in the brutal, savage things that happened to them. The world is full of horrific events, and they aren't clouds with silver linings. I'll repeat myself: sometimes life sucks. That's not to say that I don't believe that the soul is bigger than the circumstances of this lifetime, and that we can't create a beautiful, wild, amazing adventure—because I do. It's just to say that you had better own a helmet, because no matter who you are, life will hit you hard at one time or another.

Once life has hit you this way, how do you get back from being a victim to being a hero again? First, process the anger and rage, so you can make the best possible choices with the reality of your situation. Anger can be a very useful emotion when channeled into positive action. Taking responsibility for our part in the disasters that occur in life, such as divorce, bankruptcy, broken relationships, or broken bones, often empowers us to prevent similar failures. Sometimes you will encounter bad things that you have absolutely no control over, and these situations will send you into a rage. This feeling is perfectly justified in these cases, but it is still a terribly destructive emotion that can create as much pain in your life as the original event—unless you deal with it. Unfortunately, rage is a tough one. You can't meditate your way through it; you can't elevate yourself above it. The best thing you can do is own it, then transmute it through physical action. Screaming, crying, hitting pillows, boxing, and breaking plates can help—let it loose in a way that doesn't cause too much damage to anything important. If you don't find a way to transmute your rage, it will come back to haunt you.

The legacy of rage is all around us. The Old Testament speaks of the idea that "the sins of the father" can be passed on from one generation to the next. It's a sad and bitter truth. As much as I hate to admit it, you can see it demonstrated everywhere, in big and small ways. Child abusers, in many cases, grew up being abused themselves—they pass on their rage like a bad gene. Even a parent who has had a hard day at the office and then comes home to blow up at the rest of the family over something trivial is simply passing on the rage.

I was even a textbook case of passed-along rage myself. Back when I was in my early thirties, I gave one of the best presentations of my life at a convention in Las Vegas. The room was packed, and I'll never forget the people waiting to greet me off-stage and thank me for the impact I had had on their lives. Even as I was shaking hands and basking in the glow of their affection, something inside rang untrue, and I started having serious doubts. Who was I to be teaching anybody anything? I was a thirty-something guy from a well-off family who had never faced or dealt with any real struggle in his life; I was simply great at parroting Tony Robbins, Zig Ziglar, Norman Vincent Peale, and the rest of the life-coaching gurus from the past century. I remember praying, "God, let me have understanding; let me teach from a place of knowing." Well, be careful what you wish for! Over the next fifteen years, I would experience a bankruptcy, a late-stage miscarriage, a divorce, a broken back, and a shattered elbow. I would lose my sister, my daughter's mom, both parents, and along the way, be accused of a terrible crime and lose a fortune defending myself. These terrible experiences left me wiser, but they also left me with a great deal of rage.

These things happen to every adult and every family, and I don't deserve any more sympathy than any number of people you already know. The reason I'm telling you is this: I visited the sins of the father on my own family and passed along my rage instead of dealing with it. One night, I drank too much and I hurt three of the people I love the most with angry, stupid, insensitive words. The precise reasons for my behavior are irrelevant. The fact remains that I allowed my rage to transform me from the hero I want to be into a villain I don't. Unfortunately, I can never erase the memory or the action, but the good news is that I am human, I am loved by truly wonderful people, and I have opportunities to practice what I preach and work through my rage. My preferred method is boxing. When I've finished my workout, I'm ready to go out there and be a hero again.

Every day and in every moment, we are provided with a new opportunity to define ourselves: hero, villain, victim. Heroes possess the courage to have their hearts broken endlessly and never build a wall around them. This is a hero's life.

THE WORLD'S BATTLEFIELDS HAVE BEEN IN THE HEART CHIEFLY; MORE HEROISM HAS BEEN DISPLAYED IN THE HOUSEHOLD AND THE CLOSET, THAN ON THE MOST MEMORABLE BATTLEFIELDS IN HISTORY.

HENRY WARD BEECHER

Heroism Exercises

EXERCISE 1.

We have all been stopped by our fears. Our challenge for this exercise is to pay attention to that inner voice and catch it the next time it tells you, "No, you can't do that. Don't raise your hand. Don't volunteer. Don't sign up for that new class or workshop." When you catch that small, weak voice, do the opposite of what it's telling you. Remember, if you think you can't, you must. Give Worst Case Embrace a try. It works! Do something scary—step outside your box. It's a great big exciting world, and it's more fun than you think.

EXERCISE 2.

Practice heroic ownership. You are living your life—not your spouse's, not your child's, not your neighbor's. If there is something you see that's not working anywhere—your home, your company, your neighborhood, your world—fix it! Don't wait to act; do it now!

EXERCISE 3.

How are you dealing with the stress, anger, pain, and rage in your life? If you have none of these and you are older than ten, good for you (you should write your own book), but the rest of us need a plan to deal with these negative emotions. The key to getting rid of these bad feelings is transmutation, the process of changing one form of energy into another. Go out there and do something physical! I generally have my best workouts on my worst days. Whether I'm boxing or weight lifting, if I focus on any emotional pain I am experiencing and then drive that pain into the activity, two things happen: first, I am able to lift more, push harder, and go longer; and, second, I am able to release the pain, anger, and rage from my body through positive physical action.

A Psalm of Life

Tell me not in mournful numbers,
  Life is but an empty dream!
For the soul is dead that slumbers,
And things are not what they seem.

  Life is real! Life is earnest!
  And the grave is not its goal;
Dust thou are, to dust thou returnest,
  Was not spoken of the soul.

  Not enjoyment, and not sorrow,
  Is our destined end or way;
But to act, that each tomorrow
  Find us farther than today.

  Art is long, and Time is fleeting,
And our hearts, though stout and brave,
Still, like muffled drums, are beating
  Funeral marches to the grave.

In the world's broad field of battle,
  In the bivouac of Life,
Be not like dumb, driven cattle!
  Be a hero in the strife!

Trust no Future, howe'er pleasant!
Let the dead Past bury its dead!
Act,—act in the living Present!
Heart within, and God o'erhead!

Lives of great men all remind us
We can make our lives sublime,
And, departing, leave behind us
Footprints on the sand of time;

Footprints, that perhaps another,
  Sailing o'er life's solenm main,
A forlorn and shipwrecked brother,
  Seeing, shall take heart again.

  Let us then be up and doing,
  With a heart for any fate;
Still achieving, still pursuing,
  Learn to labor and to wait.

HENRY WADSWORTH LONGFELLOW

I

<u>IMAGINATION</u>

Your personal key to infinite power, possibility, and potential.

Youth is buried right next to Imagination;
when you lose one the other dies!

I HAD FLOWN to Big Bear Airport, in the mountains northeast of Los Angeles, with a friend. He was having the dashboard in his twin-engine Cherokee replaced and asked me to come along. I had never flown in a small plane before, but this kind of trip is well known to pilots for its hundred-dollar burgers, that is, when you pay five bucks for a burger and ninety-five for aircraft fuel and flight time. After lunch, the dash was finished, and we were headed home. Californians know and love these magic winter days; it had rained for a week, leaving the sun brilliant and the skies clear. We must have had seventy-five miles of visibility or better. We quickly got to our cruise altitude of about 9,500 feet, and the fog over the California coast to our West looked like a line of cotton balls. As the sun began to set, my friend grinned and asked if me I wanted to fly the plane myself. I said, "Sure!" and took the right side controls. After a while, he managed to convince me that I didn't have to grip the controls quite so hard, and I relaxed and began to have fun. He had a Vivaldi concerto playing on the sound system, and I danced to the music with the plane. If you have never been blessed with a similar experience, imagine the joy a dolphin must feel swimming in and out of a ship's wake, and you'll get the idea. For me, this was a defining moment. I knew I had to fly, and I would share the gift of flight with others I loved.

But there were some complications. With a new wife, a new home, and a new business, I could never afford to learn to fly, but I could afford a flying magazine. Four months later, I earned my private pilot's certificate. All it took was some imagination.

Imagination at Play

Imagination is the birthplace of all creation, and the most creative people can turn imagination into reality. Walt Disney called the crew that first envisioned the amazing rides at Disneyland "Imagineers," and that's still the name they use for members of their design team—but I think that there are imagineers everywhere! Young imagineers are responsible for all of the invisible friends, wild animals, cowboys and Indians, cops and robbers, and knights and dragons playing in your backyard and under your kitchen table. Older imagineers are responsible for the moon walk, the space shuttle, cruise ships, theme parks, cell phones, Starbucks, and every great book you have ever read. Imagineers are experts at creating something from nothing! They love to think, play with ideas, and create new realities, new solutions, and new directions for the world.

Our imaginations are working around the clock, but they're not always doing what's best for us. Most of our fear, worry, stress, and anxiety can be attributed to our time-traveling imagination. We travel back in time to relive old hurts and misdeeds or forward into the future to visualize terrible things that might come to pass. Extensive research has demonstrated that our nervous systems are unable to differentiate between a real and vividly imagined experience. That's why you should deal with unpleasant tasks as soon as you can—delaying them only prolongs the pain. Shakespeare's famous line from *Julius Caesar*, "A coward dies a thousand deaths, the valiant taste death but once," also addresses this phenomenon. The coward constantly visualizes the worst and relives it over and over again; the hero focuses on the task at hand, so the worst that can happen is dying only once!

Imagination can do a lot to people, in both positive and negative ways. Here's my negative example: Years ago (back when I owned a chain of martial arts schools), I placed a very good friend in charge of our largest facility. She was an exceptional teacher, but at this point in her career, she wasn't ready to run the entire operation, and it was failing. Putting her in that position was my mistake, not hers. She was a close friend; she had a small child; I knew she needed a manager's salary—but it wasn't working. I knew I had to fire her, but I kept delaying the inevitable because I kept imagining how painful it would be. In the end, the delay was all a waste—she knew she was failing, and staying in the job caused her a ton of unnecessary stress. By postponing the inevitable, I cost our company thousands of dollars. I was getting sick from the stress myself, and when I finally told her she was fired, the stress ended for all of us—I should have done it months before.

Here's my positive example: When people ask me about my religion, I tell them I'm a Muirist. I am a deeply spiritual individual, and I practice my faith the same way John Muir, the famous conservationist, did. I live by my summation of his philosophy: if I am to worship God, I shall do so in the house that he built. I have more than a love of nature; it is my sanctuary. When I am immersed in the backcountry, I feel a profound sense of peace, love, and tranquility. I even begin feeling the sense of joy that I get on my journeys into the backcountry days before the trip itself. As I plan the routes, visualize the terrain, and check my pack list, my imagination makes me feel as if I were there already, giving me a sense of joy almost as pure as what I experience on the trip itself.

Like all sources of great power, the imagination requires control, focus, and discipline. When mindfully directed, it can give you love, happiness, abundance, and adventure. When unfocused, it can run wild, wreaking havoc on our lives. Weak or strong, happy or sad, rich or poor—the way we imagine ourselves consistently will ultimately become reality.

WORDS OF GREAT POWER: "I AM."

I am powerful; I am tired; I am strong; I am ugly; I am rich; I am good; I am poor; I am cruel; I am young.

What are you? The incredible thing about the words *I am* is how many different *I am*'s there are! Take a second and reread the preceding sentence. Think about the role shifts we make in a twenty-four-hour period. How many of your *I am*'s have been mindfully imagined, and how many *I am*'s are simply thought accidents? Is life great, or is it terrible? Is the cup full, or is it empty? Is the world kind, or is it cruel? The answer to all of these questions is ultimately determined by your imagination.

Albert Einstein used his imagination as a key to unlock the mysteries of our universe. During his most productive years, the vast majorities of his theories were developed and tested with what he called mind experiments. Decades later, as the technology was developed to physically test his principles, scientists were awed at the accuracy of his "imagined tests."

IMAGINATION IS MORE IMPORTANT THAN KNOWLEDGE.
KNOWLEDGE IS LIMITED. IMAGINATION ENCIRCLES THE WORLD.

ALBERT EINSTEIN

Growing Your Imagination

Of all the strengths and skills we develop, none has a greater level of impact on the results we achieve than the imagination. We cultivate imagination through exposure to as many ideas, civilizations, concepts, histories, and teachings as possible. The easiest way to grow your imagination is through reading. An author may create an entire world with interesting characters and complex plots, but we are responsible for breathing life, color, and emotion into the words. No two people imagine the same book exactly the same way; when we read, we become co-creators and exercise our imaginations. Reading is especially good for this kind of exercise—we imagine more from words than we do from the images we see in movies and television, and its range is far broader.

The more your imagination has been exposed to different worlds and ideas, the more easily it can help you see yourself in new places and new ways. The more clearly you can see yourself as a pilot, a teacher, an entrepreneur, or a hero, the easier it will be for you to make these creative visions a reality. We all daydream, but there is a profound difference between a daydream and a creative visualization, a process I'll explain shortly. Daydreams contain little or no creative energy; they are simply distractions from the task at hand. When you use creative visualization, you plant the seed of a new reality in your mind. The more emotion and intention you can pour into your imagination, the more powerful it becomes. It's not enough to see the goal as having been completed or the skill achieved. You have to feel it, own it, and get your body to experience the joys of its newfound strengths. It is the level of the e-motional (energy in motion) commitment to a creative visualization that determines if and when you will be able to manifest it.

Once you have completed your goal-setting exercise and are clear on the things you want to be, have, or do, the next step is creative visualization. First, engage in a centering meditation to quiet the mind and release all the stress, distractions, and worries of the day. Then, with as much color, emotion, detail, and passion as your imagination can bring you, see yourself living this wonderful new life in your mind's eye. You can do this exercise globally, so that you see every aspect of your goals achieved, or you can target it on a specific goal and invest all of your energy into visualizing yourself in possession of it. To get the greatest results from your meditations, see and feel yourself as having already accomplished the goal. If you want a beautiful, strong, healthy body, then take that body out to play in your imagination. Experience the joy of your body as you surf, ski, and play with your children. Wear the clothes you have always wanted to wear, and feel comfortable in them. Take as much time as you need with the visualization, and understand that this is not a rational exercise—you are creating an alternate reality.

Every time I have experienced great success in my life is has been attached directly to the level of emotional commitment I have invested in the goal. It's never enough to want it. You must be it!

FAR AWAY IN THE SUNSHINE ARE MY HIGHEST ASPIRATIONS. I MAY NOT
REACH THEM, BUT I CAN LOOK UP AND SEE THEIR BEAUTY, BELIEVE IN THEM,
AND TRY TO FOLLOW WHERE THEY LEAD.

LOUISA MAY ALCOTT

Imagination Exercises

EXERCISE 1.

To arm your imagination, select one of the goals that you are most committed to achieving. It can be anything: losing weight, improving a relationship,
remodeling your home, controlling your finances, or lowering your golf score.
Within the next twenty-four hours, find a book, DVD, magazine, or website
created by an expert in that field. Experts in every field are waiting to help you
achieve your goal—go out and find them.

EXERCISE 2.

When planning your schedule this week, budget time for study and meditation. Set aside three blocks of time lasting forty-five minutes each. Spend at
least thirty minutes studying the material you acquired in Exercise 1. Do a
five-minute centering exercise, then spend ten minutes living your newfound
dream.

I Wandered Lonely as a Cloud

I wander'd lonely as a cloud
That floats on high o'er vales and hills,
When all at once I saw a crowd
A host, of golden daffodils;
Beside the lake, beneath the trees,
Fluttering and dancing in the breeze.

Continuous as the stars that shine
And twinkle on the Milky Way,
They stretch'd in never-ending line
Along the margin of a bay:
Ten thousand saw I at a glance,
Tossing their heads in sprightly dance.

The waves beside them danced, but they
Out-did the sparkling waves in glee:
A poet could not but be gay
In such a jocund company:
I gazed—and gazed—but little thought
What wealth the show to me had brought:

For oft, when on my couch I lie
In vacant or in pensive mood,
They flash upon that inward eye
Which is the bliss of solitude;
And then my heart with pleasure fills,
And dances with the daffodils.

WILLIAM WORDSWORTH

J
<u>JOY</u>

Experiencing peace, gratitude, happiness, and contentment simultaneously.

As a boy, I chased the illusion of happiness in things and events, always running and hiding from sadness and pain. As a man, I realize that to know Joy we must have enough courage to walk the entire path God and the universe have laid at our feet.

AT ONE TIME, I looked like a perfect product of the "me generation," but underneath it all, I felt a great deal of conflict between the lessons my Depression-reared parents wanted to pass on to me and those I had learned from my peers. My parents talked about "needs"; my friends and I talked about "wants." In 1984, I came right out of college and gladly hopped aboard the "wants" train. I wanted a home in the suburbs, a fancy car, an elegant watch, and top-shelf scotch, so I chased it all and charged it when I couldn't afford it. Ten years on that train took me to the land of divorce, bankruptcy, and ruined health. As my life fell apart, I found myself spending more of my time in nature, and in retrospect, I'm sure it was my soul's way of healing. The moment I set foot on a trail, I stopped wanting anything. For days at a time, everything I desired came from nature and the pack on my back. None of the "stuff" I had collected had any value or use in nature. As my healing continued, I found myself questioning the values I had learned while chasing all that stuff. How was it that I could find so much joy in nature and so little joy in my life with all those things? The answer surprised me, and it came from an unexpected direction.

As a martial artist, I had a deep appreciation for mastery, which I define as economy of motion, that is, getting maximum results with minimum effort. A master martial artist guides events and energy instead of fighting against them. Bruce Lee described this concept as "less is more," but what does that mean in the outdoors? Nature itself cannot be mastered—if you build a weatherproof, climate-controlled box, all you've done is banish the weather and lost nature along the way. Still, I might not be able to overcome nature itself, but I could master my wilderness skills. Doing so would involve learning to flow with nature's seasons and moods, leaving no trace of my passage, and using only enough clothing and equipment to keep myself safe and warm while maintaining an intimate connection with my surroundings. That's a big task, but I knew the rewards of developing these skills would be profound. Exactly how much knowledge and equipment would I need to live and travel in the wild? The answer turned out to be simple: a great deal of knowledge and very few possessions. With this understanding, I discovered the inverse relationship between possessions and joy. The less I carried, the farther I could travel, and the more beauty and joy I could experience. For that reason, every item in my pack had to be justified for purpose, weight, and versatility. After twenty years of trial, error, and experience, I learned that all I really need is about seven pounds of gear, along with two pounds of food per day and some water, usually provided by nature. With my seven pounds of gear, I am completely warm, well fed, and comfortable in snow, rain, hail, sunshine, and temperatures ranging from fifteen to one hundred degrees. What began as a personal challenge morphed into a philosophy that has allowed me to experience more joy than I had dreamed possible. I feel I now understand the difference between my needs and my wants.

Joy at Play

Joy comes from a full and healthy heart. It can't be purchased, manipulated, or faked; it simply is. Joy has a texture and depth that far exceeds being happy or having fun. Just as the good can be the enemy of the great, chasing happiness can limit our ability to experience joy, when we are fully present in moments of deep connection. Life in our present culture is moving so fast that we are constantly being forced out of the moment and into the future. If all we do is hurry up and get more stuff, we will never find joy. Our wants have become addictions, pulling us further away from the very things we truly need. We have formed addictions to almost everything: shopping, drugs, alcohol, exercise, television, sports, and even the Internet. All of these addictions distract us from the real joys of the human experience.

One goal of our weekly centering meditations is to help you slow down and reconnect with here and now. Learn to rediscover peace and joy in the simplest of things: breathing, feeling the warmth of the sun on your skin, or sensing a cool breeze on a summer day. Be grateful for your body—if you are still here, then all of your immediate needs have already been met. Avoid confusing the things you want with the things that you need.

You don't need ten pairs of designer shoes, a television in every room, a 15,000 square-foot house, or a car for each day of the week. Your deepest joys won't be found in any catalog or on the Home Shopping Network. Your deepest joys are found in the most quiet places—the knowledge that your family is safe and loved. Joy lives in many places: a sunrise walk on the beach, a mountain trail with the wildflowers in bloom, or your home. It comes from many experiences too: doing a kindness for your fellow man, teaching your daughter how to ride a bike or play catch, holding your wife's hand, creating something of value to share with others, or expressing love freely to those you care about. Joy is never far from us.

TO HAVE JOY ONE MUST SHARE IT. HAPPINESS WAS BORN A TWIN.

LORD BYRON

Growing Joy

Joy will not grow in the presence of greed, envy, jealousy, and want, and it grows differently for each person. Some find it in contributions to worthy causes; others find it in creativity or service to others; many find it in loving others or simply being quiet. With awareness and observation, you can come to a better understanding of your own joy. Look into the heart of things you love the most. When you have discovered the seeds of your joy, care for them like a master gardener. Avoid the two worst enemies of joy: consumption for its own sake and the fear of being still and quiet. Understand that our culture is actively working against your joy. We have created five-hundred-page magazines made up almost exclusively of ads. Your mail is literally buried under a stack of catalogs, each promising to help you become more beautiful, popular, and sexy if you only buy what they are selling. The message coming from all sides is clear: buy and you will be beautiful; buy and you will be happy; buy and you will be popular; buy and all of your pain will go away.

There is no joy to be found in consumption. At best, you will experience a short-term buzz followed by a drain in your bank account, more clutter in your home, and an almost insatiable need to go out and buy again. What you're really spending is far more precious than money—it's time. We will spend every day, every hour, every moment on some activity. How much of your time do you spend on people and activities that bring you joy? How much of your time do you spend on things that ultimately have no meaning whatsoever? Over the years, I've seen far too much time squandered, especially in the pursuit of material gain. We need to remember that everything we purchase, everything we consume, and every hour we spend takes our energy—are we using these resources wisely? I have lost my sister, my daughter's mom, and both parents in the last five years—these terrible losses have given me a big opportunity to reflect on how I spend my life. I intend to receive the greatest return on every precious hour of life I have left—no matter how many or few there may be.

Working as an executive coach, I was horrified at the number of brilliant men and women trading in their lives and joys for a nonexistent dream. Many top executives are working sixty to eight-five hour weeks—far too many hours to live anything like a reasonable, fulfilling life. If you ask them why they work so many hours, most will tell you that they're doing it for their families. They spend the vast majority of their adult lives killing themselves to add a quarter point to the company's stock value, but along the way they sacrifice their health and families. Think about the divorce, stroke, and cancer rates of our business leaders. As you reflect on how you intend to spend your life, remember that a child doesn't experience joy by counting the number of square feet in their home or comparing car and clothing logos with the neighbors. Children experience joy by having mom and dad at the baseball game, at the piano recital, along for a walk or a bike ride with them. Our children experience joy when we spend time with them—and it's never wasted that way.

Having a soul passion, loving what you do, and loving the people around you are all vital to the growth of joy. If you love cars, buy one you like; if you love flying, get a plane. But don't get them just because your neighbors have something you don't—spend your time and your life wisely.

HAPPINESS LIES IN THE JOY OF ACHIEVEMENT
AND THE THRILL OF CREATIVE EFFORT.

FRANKLIN D. ROOSEVELT

Joy Exercises

EXERCISE 1.

Learn to live in gratitude. Start by taking exactly two minutes to write down as many things as possible that bring you joy. This is my list; yours, of course, will be different.

A smile on my wife's face, and the sparkle in her eyes.
Memories of my mom and dad holding hands.
Anytime my daughter Miranda performs.
Any time I hear Robin and Kayla singing with the baby.
Everything the baby does—well, almost.
My Sunday cup of coffee, when all the family is home and Robin is making pancakes.
Being one of about ten people a year who ever set foot on my favorite trail.
Catching the new day's sunshine reflecting off a mountain stream.
Sharing something of benefit with someone, and watching their gears click and the lights come on.
Learning almost anything; teaching almost anything.
Sitting on my parent's porch, having a glass of wine, and watching the grass change color.
Sitting on my porch with close friends, and doing the same thing.
Watching people who do something well, do their thing.
Experiencing nature in all her states.

EXERCISE 2.

Keep a journal of moments that give you joy. This week, record at least one moment of joy each day. Send them to me, Share@BillPoett.com, so I can share your joy with others.

EXERCISE 3.

The next time you are about to buy something you don't need, stop and go for a thirty-minute hike in one of your favorite nature spots, and see which feels better.

A Moment of Happiness

A moment of happiness,
you and I sitting on the verandah,
apparently two, but one in soul, you and I.
We feel the flowing water of life here,
you and I, with the garden's beauty
and the birds singing.
The stars will be watching us,
and we will show them
what it is to be a thin crescent moon.
You and I unselfed, will be together,
indifferent to idle speculation, you and I.
The parrots of heaven will be cracking sugar
as we laugh together, you and I.
In one form upon this earth,
and in another in a timeless sweet land.

RUMI

K

KNOWLEDGE

*Information acquired through direct
experience, observation, or
association.*

KNOWLEDGE BY ITSELF IS USELESS; ONLY CONSISTENT, POSITIVE
APPLICATION CAN TRANSMUTE KNOWLEDGE INTO POWER AND WISDOM.

WE WERE BORN to learn, as anyone with a toddler running around the house knows. I love watching how much and how quickly we learn when we know so little. As we grow into adults, what happens to that quick, brilliant, inquisitive mind that we once had? Occasionally, we come across people who have held on to their childlike wonder for learning new things and experiencing new adventures, but far more frequently, we are forced to spend our days with those who have long since lost their joyful thirst for knowledge. The other day, Robin and I took Becca, our two-year-old, for a hike. She rode in a backpack and sang for most of the trip, but toward the end she walked along with us. While we adults were thinking about what was next on our schedule, Becca picked up rocks, twigs, and leaves and examined each of them, getting gleefully lost in the experience. She is a great teacher for her parents, and for everyone else, too.

I belong to the school board in our small town, and I'm also an educator. I understand and appreciate the challenges our teachers face, but I can't put into words the frustration I experience watching children enter our school systems with an insatiable thirst for knowledge and then seeing their spirits slowly crushed. They turn from natural learners to prisoners in a process they must endure. I know this sounds harsh, but far too many of our kids can't wait to start school, and within a very short, they time can't wait to get out!

I realized this had happened to me by the sixth grade. We were told to learn the names of each state and its capital. When I asked why, our teacher responded with a curt, "Because you have to." From that point forward, it became a game; I would get the grades needed with the least amount of effort necessary, and I would get out as soon as I could. It would take me almost twenty years to have my love of learning re-ignited, and that was thanks to a severe injury. Trapped in a bed with a fractured back, well before laptops and computer games, I was forced to read, and read I did. I consumed wisdom literature from all over the world, as well as anything and everything I could get my hands on. What a gift! The love of learning once again burned within me. I feel sorry for every child that has had the spark of curiosity extinguished and no one in their lives to help them re-ignite it!

Knowledge at Work

I have had issues with knowledge for a very long time. I guess it stems from far too many years coaching brilliant, well-educated people who are as confused, sad, and lonely as everyone else. It's quite possible that knowing as much as they do and still feeling lost actually adds to their burden. I am convinced that our culture places far too much emphasis on the accumulation of knowledge and far too little emphasis on the ability to experience joy and gratitude on a regular basis.

To help illustrate this point, I have created an enlightenment continuum, a fancy name for a way of describing the full spectrum of knowledge as part of a much greater process.

The continuum looks like this:

- **Curiosity** leads us to **seeking.**
- **Seeking** leads us to **knowledge.**
- **Knowledge** leads us to **skill.**
- **Skill** leads us to **experience.**
- **Experience** leads us to **judgment.**
- **Judgment** leads us to **wisdom.**
- **Wisdom** leads us back to **curiosity.**

When you examine this continuum, you can see how and where knowledge fits into a much greater personal-development process. If you place too much emphasis on acquiring knowledge without understanding where it belongs on this continuum, you might fail to see that it is simply one step on the path to a fully actualized life.

For instance, how often have you heard that knowledge is power? Well, pardon me for saying so, but what a load of crap. Every one of us knows something that we could start or stop doing right now that would be of great benefit to ourselves and families. Why don't we act on the knowledge we possess? The reason is simple: at our current level of personal development, we lack the discipline and the wisdom needed to drive us to action. On a carton of cigarettes the warning clearly states that smoking is bad for your health, yet people start smoking every day. There isn't an overweight American who doesn't know that they need to eat less and move more, and yet we have never been fatter as a country. Everyone understands how inexpensive a cab is and how dangerous drinking and driving are, yet every Saturday night, I bet you can think of at least one person you know who doesn't act on this knowledge.

Now don't get me wrong—I don't want to slam knowledge, I only want to put it in perspective. I have coached many men and women who have become trapped in their quest for knowledge, literally spending their lives studying things and collecting information like old postage stamps, all the while forgetting to live. Knowledge is great; just don't forget what it's for.

Knowledge can be an amazing tool. Nothing can accelerate time and move you faster toward your goals then access to the best information, techniques, and teachers. Since time is a priceless, irreplaceable asset, any tool that moves you toward your dreams and desires is invaluable. The thing to remember is that knowledge is a tool whose value lies only in its application. Today, we have greater access to knowledge than at any point in history. With a few finger strikes on a keyboard, you can pull up almost the entire work of human information. You can receive instruction through every form of media by the very best teachers in the world. If there is anything that you want to do in this lifetime, you simply need to go out and grab the knowledge and begin applying it today.

Knowledge is valueless when it is not used or is inappropriately applied; knowledge is priceless when we use it to speed us to our goals.

A WISE MAN LEARNS BY THE MISTAKES OF OTHERS, A FOOL BY HIS OWN.

LATIN PROVERB

Growing Knowledge

I sincerely believe that you are a miracle. If we were to look at all of the events that had to transpire to bring you into being, we would get some idea of your importance to the universe. That's one of the reasons I enjoy celebrating birthdays so much. They give us a chance to remember what a gift we are to the world, and they help us recommit to using that gift in the best ways possible. Having spent the better part of twenty years studying human potential, I can tell you that yours is practically unlimited. It extends as far as your imagination and your ability to gather and retain knowledge can go.

Never settle for mediocrity. Throughout my adult life, I have always made sure that when it comes to gathering knowledge, I will do everything possible to get access to the very best. As a martial artist, that meant years of flying all over the world, knocking on many doors, and never accepting no for an answer. I always intend to study with the best and make sure that the men and women I study with are actually living what they teach. If you are teaching it, you had better be living it. Be a product of the product! I have no interest in reading a book on relationships written by someone who has been divorced five times.

When you seek knowledge, never take what you get at face value. Question everything, test everything, and challenge everything. Far too much of what is being taught today has little value. I witnessed women's self-defense courses taught all over the country with countless demonstrations of completely worthless material being accepted as gospel. This practice exists in every discipline, from the martial arts to business to health and fitness! Because someone, somewhere, sometime, wrote something down doesn't make it true. Every piece of information we receive has been distorted and inter-preted to some extent, even when it comes from the best of sources—and a lot of sources aren't any good at all.

Great education will teach you how to think, not what to think. Be very afraid of anyone who professes to know and teach the absolute truth. Com-mit yourself to becoming a seeker of truth, and in this you will find freedom. It's ironic how many people have heard this and never question anything in their lives—including, at times, me!

Truth at best is elusive. Was George Washington a hero or a terrorist? Do you remember learning about the Christmas Eve attack on a British fort, where the celebrating troops were slaughtered? Because America won the war, George Washington shall be remembered for all time as a hero and the father of our country. Had the British won the war, George Washington would be nothing more than a footnote in history, the traitor hung for his evil actions!

Are you aware that there are over thirty thousand registered diets today, each claiming to be the best way to lose weight? According to the New Eng-land Journal of Medicine and every other reliable source I have ever found, the only time any of these programs work are when participants eat less and move more. Do we really need thirty thousand ways to be told that?

To grow knowledge effectively and consistently, practice the following:

+ Review your life goals and determine what knowledge you are lacking.
+ Do an online search for experts, websites, chat rooms, and instruc-tional materials.
+ At a minimum, find three qualified sources.
+ Challenge the information; look for industry, student, and cus-tomer reviews.
+ Begin applying and testing the information immediately.
+ Make sure you are enjoying the learning process.
+ Whenever possible, find a friend to share the learning adventure with.
+ Make sure you are putting your knowledge to work. Remember, knowledge is only power when it is consistently applied!

KNOWLEDGE WILL FOREVER GOVERN IGNORANCE;
AND PEOPLE WHO MEAN TO BE THEIR OWN GOVERNORS,
MUST ARM THEMSELVES WITH THE POWER WHICH KNOWLEDGE GIVES.

JAMES MADISON

Knowledge Exercises

EXERCISE 1.

Think about the knowledge you've acquired from the previous chapters in this book. You should be experiencing greater levels of joy, health, and abundance in your daily life. This chapter's assignment is to go back and review these tips for one more piece of knowledge that you could really use right now, and then apply it. It's in there somewhere—I promise!

The Thanksgiving Ham!

This was the first Thanksgiving on which Becky was going to help her mother prepare dinner. At six, she was already demonstrating a curiosity and intellect far beyond her years. She carefully watched her mother, helping when she could, and asking questions about the importance of each step in the process. Her mother took the beautiful Thanksgiving ham, her favorite part of the meal, and cut off both ends before putting it in the pot, Becky asked, "Mama, why do we do that?" Her mother, being very honest, told Becky, "I'm not really sure; it's just the way my mother taught me."

Well, this was not an answer Becky could live with, so they got on the phone and called Grandma. The answer Grandma gave was every bit as frustrating. She had always done it this way because that's how her mother had taught her. There was only one thing left to do, call Great-grandma. When they finally got her on the phone, Becky asked, "Great-grandma, how come you cut both ends off the Thanksgiving ham before you cook it?" Great-grandma's response was one that made them all laugh and cry, "Why, we were very poor and had a very small stove and pot, so we had to cut the ends off the ham to make it fit!"

What are you doing in your life because of something someone told you to do without telling you why?

L
<u>LOVE</u>

The act of caring for, protecting, enjoying, and honoring the people, places, and things we value the most.

To miss a chance to Love is to miss the point of life!

SPRING 1992, THREE o'clock in the morning: My wife is sick, I have to catch a flight at six, and here I am changing my baby's diaper. I'm twenty-nine years old, cleaning Miranda poop off both of us, when it hits me like a freight train: my parents love me way more than I could have ever imagined. I'm standing there in the nursery, rocking the baby back to sleep, and thinking about all the changes in life we have made and will continue to make for Miranda. Some people call them sacrifices, but that word doesn't feel right. I will gladly do anything for this tiny being I'm holding in my arms, just as my parents did for me. I won't do it out of any sense of obligation; I will do it because I never knew a heart could be this full. I will do it because I love her!

Why do we have to have a child of our own before we can realize the depth of our parents' love for us? Those thoughts and feeling never leave me. In 2009, as I watched Miranda, seventeen, drive away from home, I thought of myself as a teenager and all the sleepless nights I caused my mom. I wish I could just hold my mom one more time and apologize for my thoughtlessness, tell her I finally understand, and that I know her love for me.

Fall 2008: My dad's body is slowly succumbing to the cancer. Watching helplessly as it steals a little more of his strength every day is one of the hardest things I have ever done. I lift him into the shower, an act which is no great feat because of his weight loss, and I proceed to wash and shave him. I know how humiliating this is for a man of his pride, but I also know how much better he will feel when we're done. Although his body is failing him, his mind is as sharp as ever, and he won't stop apologizing for the burden he believes he is placing on his family. It becomes a daily ritual: he apologizes, and I tell him that there is no greater privilege for a son than to have a chance to care for the man who spent his whole life caring so tenderly for his own wife and children. It's funny that it was really hard for my dad to say he loved me when I was growing up, though he demonstrated it in a thousand ways. Toward the end of his life, as there was less he could physically do to demonstrate his love, he finally found the words and used them all the time. I love you, too, Pop.

Love at Work

Until you can learn to love yourself well, don't expect to experience great love from others. Even after twenty years of doing different kinds of coaching, I'm still surprised by the amount of negative self-talk I hear from clients. "I'm not coordinated." "I'm fat." "I can't do that." "I'm no good at this." The stream of negative thoughts is endless. If this is what they really think, it's no wonder so many people can't spend time alone.

To achieve what you really want, you have to turn these negative thoughts around. The one trait that most consistently separates super-achievers from under-achievers is the quality of their most significant relationship: the one they have with themselves. Super-achievers have a great respect, admiration, and love for themselves; underachievers don't. Keep in mind that when I talk about self-love, I don't mean conceit. Conceit is a petty emotion held by small-minded people who feel a need to see themselves as superior to others. Self-love is simply an acknowledgment of all the gifts of being human. It brings a joy in the nurturing, development, and expression of these gifts. Men and women with a healthy sense of self-love find loving others only natural, because the gifts they posses are so easily seen and appreciated in others.

Nurture the relationship you have with the one person you can never escape or deceive for any length of time: you. Remember, you spend every conscious moment listening and talking with yourself. The quality of your life is wrapped up in your feelings about who you are.

Embrace the gift of yourself, and the rest will come much more easily. Nurturing and developing something out of sheer discipline is difficult; doing these things out of love is easy. Have you ever seen those classic cars driving through town on a Sunday afternoon? Think of the love and care that goes into restoring and maintain those beauties. You can see the payback on the grins of their drivers as they cruise through town. Wouldn't it be great if we could get the same level of joy, pride, and satisfaction from taking care of our bodies, minds, and spirits? Have you ever seen the horse trailers, grooms, tack, trainers, and supplements a race horse receives? We, on the other hand, skip meals, eat whatever junk (and I mean it, it's really junk!) is lying around, work too hard, stress too much, sleep poorly, and expect our bodies to do the impossible with little or no maintenance. Then we bitch when we don't feel well or get sick. Come on—where's the love in that?

Imagine yourself as the most beautiful, powerful, amazing machine ever created—and imagine that you come with a user's guide, too. What would the guide tell you about proper care and use of your machine? What are some things you would need to do to get a lifetime of play, joy, and use out of you?

Now, what if every member of your family, all of your friends, and the people surrounding you, were machines of equal magnificence? How would that change your relationships with them?

At the heart of self-love is a profound understanding of your unique value as a human being. With this understanding comes a divine charge to nurture, develop, and enjoy your gifts for as long as you can. When you truly embrace your own worth and can love yourself without reservation, then you can't help but see the beauty and value in everyone around you. You begin to see all that is right in people, instead of all that is wrong. It becomes less of a bother and more of a blessing to care for and honor yourself and all those around you. If you can truly see yourself as a beautiful, amazing, powerful child of the creator, then how can you not love all of his children?

THERE IS ONLY ONE HAPPINESS IN LIFE, TO LOVE AND BE LOVED.

GEORGE SAND

Growing Love

I'm sure many of you are thinking, "OK, this sounds great on paper, but the truth is, I hate my body, and I can't stand my neighbor. I read the newspaper, watch TV, and listen to the conversations at the coffee stations, and—to be totally honest—I find very little that is lovable about anybody. Even in my life, I seem to fail more often than I succeed; I get angry with myself and others; I say and do stupid things. I am certainly not living the life of a beautiful, powerful, amazing machine."

Welcome to one of the greatest challenges of your life—overcoming the fact that these observations are fundamentally true. If love is essential to our joy and happiness, and self-love is at the crux of this, how do we learn to love ourselves and those around us when we all engage in so many unlovable acts? That's a great question!

To borrow a bit of wisdom from Buddhism, all pain and all suffering is a direct result of placing expectations upon yourself and others. It's the consequence of wanting people and things to be the way we want them to be, instead of the way they are. Learning to remove these expectations is one of the first steps in freeing ourselves and finding love. We constantly place expectations upon the ones we love, and when they fail to meet these expectations, we become angry and frustrated. Then we begin to act on this anger and frustration by withholding our love, and a negative spiral begins. The back-and-forth struggle about what we should or shouldn't have done becomes a horrible dance, and soon, the withholding of love becomes a weapon in a perverse power struggle that is anything but loving.

Think back to when you fell in love. Did you act in a loving way because it was expected of you, or because of the joy it brought you? Like sunshine and water to a plant, these loving, unselfish acts of yours created the love you experienced. Somewhere along the way, the dynamic of your relationship changed, and you began to do things because your expectations were met, instead of doing them as a natural expression of your love. This is the point where love becomes bartering, and it's not pretty. I can't tell you how many times I've heard, "I'm just not in love anymore." Well, of course you're not! You can't stop performing loving actions and maintain love any more than you can stop exercising and maintain fitness.

As we evolve, we can act out of love as a personal choice rather than as a response to the actions of others. Loving thoughts, words, and deeds are the highest form of self-expression. They flow from our beautiful, magnificent machine when it is operating as it was intended. They are never based on an equal and opposite response from the people around us. Still, I'm not suggesting that we walk around constantly in a blissed-out state; it isn't possible, appropriate, or honest. There will be times when feeling angry, frustrated, confused, or upset is simply the right way to feel. We must honor the full range of human emotion if we are to remain honest and alive. According to my sources, even the Dalai Lama, one of the most loving, compassionate people on earth, can lose his temper at times.

Growing love is about consciously acknowledging your tremendous value and the value of all those around you. This acknowledgement will drive you to take better care of yourself and everyone else too. Acting from love is always our highest choice. Learn to ask and answer the question, "What would love do now?" This question can be applied to any situation—from ordering lunch at a fast food restaurant to the best way to deal with your child's temper tantrum. The human brain is hard wired to find answers to the questions we ask. Consistently ask this question of yourself, and you will be awed by your own wisdom: what would love do now?

I understand, in your eyes your body is far from perfect, but what would anyone confined to a wheelchair not give for a healthy body?

LIFE'S GREATEST HAPPINESS IS TO BE CONVINCED WE ARE LOVED.

VICTOR HUGO

Love Exercises

EXERCISE 1.
Write down nine things you love about you.

1. _____
2. _____
3. _____
4. _____
5. _____
6. _____
7. _____
8. _____
9. _____

EXERCISE 2.
List three loving actions you consistently take for yourself.

1. _____
2. _____
3. _____

EXERCISE 3.
List three loving actions you consistently take for others.

1. _____
2. _____
3. _____

EXERCISE 4.
All week, apply the "What would love do now?" question to as many scenarios as you can think of.

How Do I Love Thee?

How do I love thee? Let me count the ways.
I love thee to the depth and breadth and height
My soul can reach, when feeling out of sight
    For the ends of Being and ideal Grace.
    I love thee to the level of every day's
Most quiet need, by sun and candlelight.
I love thee freely, as men strive for Right;
I love thee purely, as they turn from Praise.
    I love with a passion put to use
In my old griefs, and with my childhood's faith.
    I love thee with a love I seemed to lose
With my lost saints,—I love thee with the breath,
Smiles, tears, of all my life!—and, if God choose,
    I shall but love thee better after death.

ELIZABETH BARRETT BROWNING

M
<u>MOTIVATION</u>

The fuel that drives all action; energy in motion.

WITHOUT MOTIVATION, DREAMS ARE LIFELESS THINGS!

WHAT DRIVES US to victory? How do we keep moving when we have nothing left to give? What separates success from failure and defeat? I'm often asked, "How can I motivate myself, my son, my daughter, my employee, or anybody?" This is a profoundly challenging question. We've all heard the expression "you can lead a horse to water, but you can't make him drink." Although this cliché has some merit, it isn't absolutely true. In fact, success often comes from the ability to motivate, inspire, and drive yourself or others to do difficult or unpleasant things, when motivation alone gets the job done. Motivating yourself or others is an elusive skill. No two people are motivated by exactly the same thing, and what motivates each of us can change over time.

Here's an example from my own experience. I had been training for a difficult hike by speed hiking the stadium steps at Santa Barbara City College wearing a forty-pound weight vest. Now, I've already mentioned that I don't really enjoy exercise; on the contrary, I find that staying motivated to work out is a constant test of my focus and discipline. Most importantly, I'm driven to exercise by the results I achieve, not because I take pleasure in it. One day, I arrived at the field and was met by bright red booths, balloons, banners, and music. The college was hosting a Special Olympics track and field day. Without paying too much attention to the event, I strapped on my weight vest, engaged my core, and began driving up the steps. By the third or fourth row of stairs my quads were beginning to burn, my heart rate was knocking on 170 beats per minute (nearly the limit for a guy my age), and I was really starting to focus on my breathing in order to maintain my pace. Basically, I was hurting, and I knew this session was going to be brutal from beginning to end. Then I happened to glance at the field just as a race was starting. Not fifty yards away, a young girl wearing two full-length leg braces was trying to run with crutches. She was being helped by a teenage boy with Down's syndrome. I froze, as I watched them push for the finish line while their family and friends cheered. The entire race lasted less than a minute, but I know it will be burned into my memory forever. As I continued with my workout, I noticed tears streaming down my cheeks, and I heard myself asking God for forgiveness. Here I was, a healthy man in the prime of his life, complaining about how much this exercise hurt. The universe gave me a chance to see true courage overcoming real pain. I finished that session in record time, and I'll remember those two amazing athletes every time I work out.

Motivation at Work

You can see motivation at work all around you. It's at work with the student you see in the library on a Friday night. It's at work with the football player who never misses a practice, always takes the field first, and leaves it last. Motivation shines in the eyes of the salesman who never gives up trying to help a customer and the mother who still stays in shape after having three kids. Hernando Cortés, the Spanish conquistador, had a genius for motivation. According to one source, after sailing his troops to confront the much larger, better equipped Aztec force, he unloaded his army and supplies and ordered the ships destroyed. As his dismayed soldiers watched their only way home run aground on the rocks, Cortés turned to his men and said, "If you ever want to see your homes and families again, we must win!" And so they did.

At the most basic level, motivation can be understood by the well-known "carrot and the stick" analogy. Imagine driving a wagon being pulled by a mule. In your right hand, you hold a carrot on a pole that dangles in front of the mule, just out of reach of his mouth. In your left hand, you hold a stick you use to smack the mule's behind. The mule is motivated to move forward by a desire for pleasure—eating the carrot—and to avoid pain—being hit by the stick. Research has shown that the desire to avoid pain is usually the more powerful of the two motivations. But I have railed against this apparent truth for as long as I can remember.

I have always argued for my belief in the best of humanity. After all, doesn't everyone exercise, eat right, and get plenty of rest because of all the good it does us? Don't we all take 10 percent of each paycheck and place it in a savings or investment account? Don't we also donate the next 10 percent of our income to charity to help those less fortunate than we are? Of course, we don't need contracts and attorneys; our words are our bonds! Of course, none of us ever spends too much money—if we don't have it, we don't buy it!

OK, my tongue has almost poked through my cheek, but I'm sure you are all getting the point. Now, it's possible that you might know someone who does all the right things, all the time, simply because they are the right things to do. Yet, I'll bet you all of the money that hasn't quite made it into my own savings account, that almost everyone you know doesn't do all of these things consistently. Look at America's obesity, divorce, failed business, and debt rates, and you'll see that, as a nation, we aren't doing any of these things very well.

Now, if after an objective examination, you give your body, mind, spirit, finances, relationships, citizenship, and sense of humor an A grade, skip the rest of this section on motivation. If you're not yet making the dean's list in life, then please read on.

If we know that proper diet, exercise, rest, study, honoring commitments, following through, and the one hundred other lessons we are taught from childhood are important, good for us, and lead us to a better life, then why don't we do them? You may not like the answer to this question, but unfortunately, it's the truth. We often don't do what is best for us because at the moment when we make a significant, self-defining choice, we associate too much pain with the better choice, and more pleasure to the worse one. We end up acting against our long-term best interests to avoid short-term pain. Why do you think people in America smoke, while possessing the knowledge that this disgusting habit not only makes them smell bad, but is actually killing them?

Think about how many of these self-defining choices you make in a day. It's six a.m. You are supposed to go for your run, but the bed is so warm, it's so cold outside, and your foot is sore. You're at dinner and they bring out the free bread and oil. It's sitting there, staring at you, daring you to eat it. Your paycheck is deposited in your checking account, and as you're about to make that transfer into your IRA, you get a new clothing catalog—you haven't bought yourself anything new to wear in six months.

When you make a self-defining choice that isn't in your long-term best interests, you do it because at that moment, you believe that choice will bring greater pleasure and less pain than any other. That's all—it comes down to the carrot in front of you and the stick behind you. Can you do any better than that mule?

Think of motivation as the emotional driver behind your actions and inactions. You are motivated to do something or nothing, based on your personal interpretation of the cost/benefit (pain/pleasure) ratio of any action or inaction. As you begin to understand your motivations better, you will become more disciplined in your habits and develop greater control over this cost/benefit relationship. Then you can gain greater control over your daily level of motivation and make better decisions.

Why don't we all have our motivations under control already? The problem goes back a long way. Our lessons in motivation began with our parents, who offered and withheld their approval based on the things we did or didn't do. We quickly learned to associate pain and pleasure to certain consistent responses we received from those around us. These associations helped us form behavioral thresholds—that is, the boundaries of what we will or won't do—and we matured into adults who behave, more or less, the way adults do.

Even as adults, we are constrained by these deeply ingrained patterns. We seek out approval, respect, and friendships according to what we learned as children; we view our relationships with our bodies, nature, and education through the eyes of our parents' approval and disapproval. Of course, our parents had the best intentions, but what was appropriate for you as a child may not be helpful to you now. Don't you think it's time to take responsibility for your own motivations?

DO NOT WAIT TO STRIKE TILL THE IRON IS HOT;
BUT MAKE IT HOT BY STRIKING.

WILLIAM B. SPRAGUE

Growing Motivation

I know, theory is great, but I need to lose thirty pounds, start an IRA, and finish ten projects around work and home, and all I want to do is play on the computer or lay on the couch. How do I motivate myself to get started? To grow motivation in your life, you must be motivated to create change. I know, it sounds like a Catch-22, and in certain respects, that's true. How can I be motivated when I'm not? If I'm already motivated, then I don't need any more motivation. Ouch! Do you remember me saying at the beginning of this section that motivation is one of the hardest things to learn, create, and maintain? That's still the case, but we're going to do it anyway.

You might not be able to create enough motivation immediately to change your entire life, but I'm sure you can easily identify specific areas you need to improve. If you've read this book from the beginning, you've already done several exercises on personal inventories and goal setting. Right now, we're going focus on creating motivation for the most common goal of all: changing your body. The techniques we use here can be applied to any aspect of your life, but the key to making any change is beginning with a specific area. That's what we're going to do now.

The first step in attacking any problem is to remember the 10/90 rule. In other words, we apply 10 percent of our energy to identifying and defining the problem and 90 percent of our energy to creating, implementing, quantifying, and maintaining the solution.

Let's talk about your body. I hope you are madly in love with yours and appreciate it for the unbelievable machine that it is. What else can taste, touch, smell, hear, see, think, learn, laugh, run, jump, climb, ski, swim, make love, laugh, dance, create life … and I'm barely touching on all of the things your body can do. Do you wake up every morning and thank God for what you have been blessed with, and then spend a moment or two focusing on the things you will do today to honor, maintain, and care for your beautiful body?

Maybe you don't—many people have negative attitudes toward their bodies. As a trainer, you have no idea how many times I have heard very healthy men and women say, "I hate my body." If you're in this category, the first thing you have to fix on your path to growing your motivation for a healthy, beautiful, powerful, body is your attitude toward it. How could you be motivated to fix something you hate? In this culture, we hide our bodies in clothing, jewelry, shoes, cars, homes, and careers. We completely disassociate ourselves from the damage that lack of exercise, rest, and proper nutrition does to our beautiful machines. In fact, we have become so good at hiding from our bodies and so good at chemistry that we have developed pills to hide the consequences of our abuse. We take beta-blockers and cholesterol pills; we take pills for erections and pills for the depression we might experience when we accidently see ourselves naked in the mirror. We no longer accept invitations to the beach or pool parties, or if we do, we bring a tent to hide under and in. We don't take our children and grandchildren hiking, skiing, horseback riding, and camping. Instead, we take them to the movies, where we can sit and eat. We delude ourselves right up to the moment of our first heart attack, or when our loved ones find us unattractive and embarrassing.

I honestly hope reading the previous paragraph was as painful for you as writing it was for me. I also hope that none of you who are reading this have experienced, or will ever experience, any of the things I was describing. Yet, you should remember that pain is the more powerful motivator! The sad truth is the two most successful diets in America today are not Atkins and South Beach—they're the divorce and the "my doctor says I'm going to die" diet. The pain of either of these experiences is usually enough to motivate people to make pretty radical changes in their lifestyles. Why not make the possibility that these events might happen enough to change your behaviors? Then you can avoid these events instead of reacting to them.

When you want to change your body, love it, look at it, have a physical, and find out exactly what is working well, and what isn't. Even the fat that you find so unattractive on your body is nothing more than stored energy. Taking a clear, honest, clinical look at your strengths and weakness is the best place to start. Then begin looking for role models of all ages, not only people in their teens and twenties. By far, the most beautiful women I train are mothers in their forties and fifties. Their bodies are magnificent, and they go to the beach and play with their children in the water—and they wear bathing suits that teenagers might find challenging. They're having a great time and looking good doing it!

You can, too. Begin connecting the choices you make with their consequences. Each choice is important! Choose the chicken salad and daily exercise—that choice will take you to the beach and the dance. Choose the extra helping of dessert and the extra time on the couch, and that choice will take you to baggy clothes and the emergency room. Think it all the way through—associate massive pain with the negative consequences of each bad choice and allow yourself to feel joy at the positive consequences of each good choice.

The key to motivation is determining your own personal cost/benefit ratios so that they move you towards the things you most desire. Change how you interpret what is painful and what isn't. Understand that when you are faced with two pains you will move away from what you think is the greatest. The men and women who make it to the gym consistently are the ones who have learned to associate more pain to being unhealthy than the pain they experience from training and controlling their diets. Don't forget how great a day of skiing with your grandchildren will feel, or what is like being the only sixty year old at the beach still in a bathing suit, surfing with the grandkids.

IF YOUR ACTIONS INSPIRE OTHERS TO DREAM MORE, LEARN MORE, DO MORE AND BECOME MORE, YOU ARE A LEADER.

JOHN QUINCY ADAMS

Motivation Exercises

EXERCISE 1.
Write down nine things you love about your body.

1. _____
2. _____
3. _____
4. _____
5. _____
6. _____
7. _____
8. _____
9. _____

EXERCISE 2.
Write down everything not being in the best shape of your life today has cost you. What will it cost you in ten to twenty years?

_____
_____
_____

EXERCISE 3.
Write down all the things you would do and enjoy if you woke up tomorrow in a healthy, beautiful, powerful body. What would you be doing in ten to twenty years with this body? There are plenty of seventy- and eighty-year-old skiers, runners, lovers, and mountain climbers.

_____
_____
_____

EXERCISE 4.
What do you need to do differently today to change and honor your body? Write it down—and do it!

_____
_____
_____

The Road Not Taken

Two roads diverged in a yellow wood,
And sorry I could not travel both
And be one traveler, long I stood
And looked down one as far as I could
To where it bent in the undergrowth;

Then took the other, just as fair,
And having perhaps the better claim,
Because it was grassy and wanted wear;
Though as for that passing there
Had worn them really about the same,

And both that morning equally lay
In leaves no step had trodden black.
Oh, I kept the first for another day!
Yet knowing how way leads on to way,
I doubted if I should ever come back.

I shall be telling this with a sigh
Somewhere ages and ages hence:
Two roads diverged in a wood, and I—
I took the one less traveled by,
And that has made all the difference.

ROBERT FROST

N
<u>NO-THING</u>

The power of using less to create more freedom, joy, peace, and wonder in our lives.

No-thing stops me; I dare to dream!

A BACKCOUNTRY MORNING soothes the soul like nothing else. Mother Nature reaches out to all my senses there, giving me a kind of spiritual awakening. Each new day in the wild has a beautiful cadence, a visceral, musical quality. The night sounds of crickets, frogs, and owls fade away and are replaced by something much more subtle. The stream dancing by my camp keeps time, the only constant in my temporary mountain home. The morning sun peeks over the ridge and warms my body through my quilt. I become aware of a scent, primal and comforting, gently drawing me toward awareness. It's a blend of morning dew and damp, living earth, mixed with fresh wildflowers and sage. Then I hear the woodland creatures making their way through the brush to our stream for a cool first-light drink. The birds begin to sing in celebration of the new day. This natural symphony teases me until I slowly open my eyes, and without moving from my toasty cocoon, I take in the beauty and new life that is my home for the moment. The feeling of a backcountry morning always renews me, whatever the weather may be. I've experienced this awakening in the middle of a spring storm, with the dancing of rain on my tarp, and I've listened to the profound silence of a bed of virgin snow high on a mountain top.

They say that for us to survive in today's over-stimulated, information-overloaded culture, our senses actually have to become desensitized. They are forced to filter out most of what we see, hear, and feel, only allowing a tiny fraction of life's stimuli through. Daily, we are bombarded by more and more sights, sounds, information, activities, people, and clutter. This noise has become so pervasive that we are losing the ability to engage our senses actively and fully. Like a palate that has been numbed by too many strong spices, we are losing the best part of ourselves in a sea of noise.

I have renewed my ability to experience and appreciate mountain sensory magic through the power of "No-thing." In the backcountry, I sleep under the stars or a tarp that provides me with enough protection from the elements but with no walls to separate me from the wilderness. I have no phone, no schedule to keep, no e-mails to respond to, no things to buy, collect, clean, or take care of. My only responsibilities are finding water and staying warm. I carry all the clothes and shelter I need and select which natural wonders I wish to explore. The closer I come to taking no-thing with me, the greater my sense of freedom and connection. The more time I spend with no-thing, the deeper my sense of self and God become. Maybe the fact that our lives begin and end with no-thing has something to do with how good no-thing feels.

No-thing at Work

Over a five year period, I've had the opportunity to study life through encounters with death. These experiences began with my sister's death, followed by my daughter's mother's death, and ended—for now—with the death of both my parents. One thing death does well is force us to reflect on life. What does it mean? Why am I here? What matters? What doesn't? While none of these questions is new to anyone over the age of twelve, we find more depth in the reflections that are forced upon us when we lose people we care about. Like many people, I have discovered that while the answers may vary from person to person, they have a few common threads. For me, the most profound thread is the understanding that life is no-thing more or less than the conscious moments we spend each day. How well I spend these precious moments determines how much joy, beauty, and love I can manifest in them. Since we all have a limited number of moments to spend, wouldn't it make sense to use every moment as well as possible? If you were to look back on any given day and weigh the value of each moment you spent, would you be pleased?

Ask yourself some hard questions about the time you spend. What portion of your life are you spending with people you love and respect and doing things you value? What portion of your life are you spending on valueless time- and life-stealing activities?

These very important questions lead us to this performance tip: "No-thing." It is neither necessary nor valuable to have every waking moment of every day filled with some-thing, unless that some-thing is truly important to us. We all need blocks of no-thing in our daily schedules; when we are committed to no-thing, we have the ability to think, pray, meditate, heal, process, and ultimately, define who we are and how we spend our lives. We can learn to say no to more useless things—and the more we say no, the more freedom we have to spend time with the people and things that matter.

I've been invited to many A-list parties, and I've watched many breathtaking sunsets with people I care about—and I've learned which experience matters more. The joy I feel in the quiet, precious moments with Robin or my girls is worth a thousand parties with anyone else in the world. I've also learned something from coaching some of America's most affluent men and women by looking at two things: how they achieved their financial abundance and how much joy they experienced in the process. Here's my discovery: there is no correlation between those two factors: money and joy. In fact, if you look at the divorce and addiction rates of wealthy (and famous) people, you'll find that the standard definition of success has nothing to do with a person's happiness. I have, however, found a correlation between the amount of joy in someone's life and that person's ability to say no. Having a beautiful home, family, and body are totally valueless without an equal capacity to enjoy them. You would be amazed at how many people live in the most beautiful homes in the most beautiful places, yet rarely take the time to be there, because they are so busy with so many some-things!

I know—I'm busy, too. Imagine how a typical American family man's mind runs through the schedule in his head: "The alarm goes off. After a five-minute snooze, I'm up and at it by six o'clock. I hit the gym, shower, and grab a bite on the way to work. In my car, I'm listening to the news, reviewing my schedule. At the office by eight o'clock. I rifle through the Wall Street Journal, check my e-mails, make calls, and clear my desk for the nine thirty conference call. I do more, faster and better, than I did yesterday. I'm home by six thirty, grab a scotch, and kiss my kids good night."

His wife's life is just as busy: "The baby wakes up at six thirty. I've got to make lunches, dress the kids, do whatever cleaning I can, and I'm out the door for the carpool. I run to the store and catch up with friends on the way. Back home, I check e-mails, clean, do laundry while baby naps, then I pick up the kids at two thirty. Timmy's got karate; Katie has to get to dance practice on the other side of town; the baby is sick. I'm home by six thirty, grab a to-go dinner, have a glass of chardonnay, tuck in the kids." And that's a day in the life of a fairly old-fashioned couple—it's worse for single parents and people with less financial stability.

We've got to do better at doing no-thing in spite of all we've got to do. We drive ourselves at four hundred miles an hour, right to the edge of sanity and then take a vacation. Since we know no-thing but our frenzied pace, we come home from our travels exhausted and jump right back on the treadmill. When does this stop, or even slow down? At death? That's one sure way to clear a calendar!

How many of us have lost complete control of our schedules? Until you master the art of no-thing, your schedule and, for that matter, your life, will be controlled by the whims of others. Learning to say no to as many worthless things is a skill worth pursuing! As Stephen Covey (the author of the *Seven Habits* books) can tell you, being efficient and getting a lot of things done is not nearly as valuable as being effective and getting the right things done. When we embrace no-thing, free our schedules, reduce our wants, and find time to return to our true home, nature, we find healing.

DOST THOU LOVE LIFE? THEN DO NOT SQUANDER TIME, FOR THAT IS THE STUFF LIFE IS MADE OF.

BENJAMIN FRANKLIN

Growing No-thing

Why is no-thing so hard for so many people? If joy were easy, then wouldn't everyone experience it on a regular basis? To learn to live with no-thing and develop the ability to enjoy and appreciate every-thing, you must subjugate a lifetime of programming and practically every bit of feedback our "give me more" culture is throwing at you. As children, we learn to be pleasers: we get our needs met by doing certain things and forgoing other things that please other people. As adults, we often feel obligated to say yes to people and things out of that same programmed need to please. Unfortunately, we regularly say yes and fill our time with things that aren't in our best interests. Over and over, I see people constantly overbooking their schedules and taking on way too many responsibilities, simply because they are afraid to say no.

If you were to be diagnosed today with a terminal illness that would leave you with only six months of health, what would you say no to? What things, tasks, and people would you no longer tolerate in the precious time you have left? The *first* step in opening the door to "no-thing" is to acknowledge your own mortality. Understand that whether we are given twenty or one hundred years in these bodies, we will never have enough moments to experience all the amazing, beautiful, magical adventures life has waiting for us. The second step is to accept responsibility for mindfully spending your precious moments on the "things" that matter and not filling your life with wasteful some-things. The third step is to reawaken your senses and spend time in nature where you are surrounded by reminders of simple beauty and energetic harmony.

If you have come this far in our adventure together, then there are certain things I know about you. You believe in your own unique value. You are committed to making your life, and the lives of those around you, better and brighter. You are open to new thoughts and new ideas. The exercises in this performance tip can have a greater positive impact on you than any that have come before. I hope you will trust me, and invest yourself fully in the art of no-thing. If you can embrace and understand no-thing, then any-thing is possible.

IF ONE ADVANCES CONFIDENTLY IN THE DIRECTION OF HIS DREAMS,
AND ENDEAVORS TO LIVE THE LIFE WHICH HE HAS IMAGINED, HE WILL MEET
WITH A SUCCESS UNEXPECTED IN COMMON HOURS.

HENRY DAVID THOREAU

No-thing Exercises

EXERCISE 1.
Find a hiking trail near you, and say no to one activity each week so that you can get home to nature. (If you are a woman, find a friend willing to go with you, for safety's sake.) The hike should take between thirty and forty-five minutes. For fifteen minutes, travel in absolute silence. During your hike, separate from your friend by at least seven yards. Each week, during this fifteen minute section, exercise a different sense.

EXERCISE 2.
In the first week, focus on sight. Give thanks for the ability to take in all the beauty that surrounds you; then, for the next fifteen minutes, direct all your energy to your vision. Look at the trail in ways that are new to you; look at the sky and how the colors dance with each other. Get down as close as you can and consider all the love and thought that went into the creation of one flower. Change your range, and go from studying a leaf to seeing how far your sight will take you. Continue your hike, and enjoy it in the way that feels best to you.

EXERCISE 3.
In the second week, focus on sound. Give thanks for the ability to take in all the sounds that surround you; then, for the next fifteen minutes, direct all your energy to listening. Hear the trail in ways that are new to you; think of your hearing as a form of radar. Push it out in front of you as far as you can, and hold it there for a few moments. Now direct it to your right side, then behind you, and finally to the left. Create a small cone all around you, and take in as much sound as you can process. Then pick up any sounds that you find interesting. Continue your hike, and enjoy it in the way that feels best to you.

EXERCISE 4.
In the third week, focus on touch. Give thanks for the ability to feel the entire environment that surrounds you; then, for the next fifteen minutes, direct all your energy to feeling. Begin with your body, and feel your weight in each step; feel the difference in terrain as you make the transition from pavement to dirt, to grass, to stone. Feel your skin against your clothing as you walk. How does it change as your body heats up? Notice the sun and breeze against your skin. Explore all the textures around you. Pick up a flower, a rock, a twig, and revel in your body's ability to feel things. Continue your hike, and enjoy it in the way that feels best to you.

Exercise 5.

In the fourth week, focus on taste. Give thanks for the ability to taste nature; then, for the next fifteen minutes, direct all your energy into how nature tastes. (No, we are not going to eat leaves or dirt.) This is the most challenging of all the exercises, but with your sense of smell now engaged, you can actually experience different tastes in your mouth as you move along your hike. There is a subtle difference between what you taste standing next to an oak tree or a sage bush at the base of a ridge and what you taste standing at the top of a ridge. Focus on breathing in through your nose, and then direct all your energies into your sense of taste. As you move to different areas, repeat the exercise. Don't get frustrated if this takes some work as it is one of the most subtle skills to develop. Continue your hike, and enjoy it in the way that feels best to you.

Exercise 6.

Write in a journal each evening after your sensory hikes. Reflect on how your attitude has changed and how you were able to carry the wonderful experience of no-thing into other areas of your life.

Spring

See the Spring herself discloses,
And the Graces gather roses;
See how the becalmed seas
Now their swelling waves appease;
How the duck swims, how the crane
Comes from winter home again;
See how Titan's cheerful ray
Chaseth the dark clouds away;
Now in their new robes of green
Are the plowman's labors seen:
Now the lusty teeming Earth
Springs each hour with a new birth;
Now the olive blooms: the vine
Now doth with plump pendants shine;
And with leaves and blossoms now
Freshly bourgeons every bough.

ANACREON

Translated by Thomas Stanley

O
<u>OPTIMISM</u>

Living and acting with the belief that regardless of current circumstances, you will be fine.

I SEE OPTIMISM AS A MUCH MORE PROACTIVE TRAIT THEN SIMPLY "THE GLASS IS HALF FULL". I SEE OPTIMISM AS THE QUALITY THAT WILL DRIVE A MAN OR WOMEN TO FIND THE WELL, AND IF THE WELL CAN'T BE FOUND, THEN THEY WILL DAMN WELL DIG ONE!

MAYBE IT'S TWENTY years of martial arts training, or maybe it's having "of the war" (de la Guerra) as a middle name, but for as long as I can remember, I've lived my life to expect the best, while preparing for the worst.

New Year's Day 2000: I had done it! I was thirty-seven and had survived a wagon train of life's great pains. Although I was emotionally beat up, I was still standing. I won't bore you with a laundry list of the bad things that had happened to me, but about anything you could imagine had gone wrong. On that day, none of it mattered. I was driving home from the ranch in my rebuilt monster 1974 Land Cruiser, and I had a new day, a new year, and a new millennium to play with. OK, I didn't have a job, a place to live, a checking account, a cell phone, or any money in the bank, but I did have enough gas to get to my buddy's condo, where I could begin the process of rebuilding my life.

I was cruising down the coast, the sun was shining, I was grinning like a fool, when *bam*, I heard a brief but violent gun battle coming from under the hood of my car. Instantly, I started begging, pleading, and praying to the engine gods, "Just get me home." It seemed as if my prayers had been answered and the violence under my hood abated. As gingerly as possible, I continued my drive. About a half hour later on a particularly dangerous stretch of highway, I heard another enormous *bam*, then I felt a couple of violent bounces. Finally, I saw large pieces of my car skidding down the highway behind me in my rear-view mirror. I nursed the car over to the emergency lane, climbed out of the passenger door, and ran back along the highway to collect really large and important pieces of my engine. I soon realized the awful truth: my Land Cruiser was dead! Not disabled, but dead, dead, dead. I took a quick personal inventory. I had no money, no phone, no credit card, no bank account, no auto club, and I was lying under my dead cruiser on the side of the highway on New Year's morning. To use a military acronym I told you about in "B," my situation was totally fubar (f---ed up beyond all recognition).

After wallowing for a while in a puddle of self-pity, I rolled back towards the ocean and fell into a scene from the movie *Endless Summer*. Past the point, I saw a longboard surfer on the ride of his life. On January 1, a large portion of America is usually buried under snow, but on that day in Southern California, it was eighty degrees, and sparkling sun gems painted the line of a surfer's perfect wave as a light off-shore breeze sent liquid dancers into the brilliant blue sky. It was one of those perfect movie moments that makes the world both love and hate Californians. I was lying under my broken truck on the side of the freeway with literally nothing, yet I was as happy as I can remember. I started laughing (OK, I might have had a small breakdown at this point), but like the rider on his wave, I knew everything was going to be OK.

Optimism at Work

All of us will certainly experience pain, illness, loss, and eventually, death. On the other hand, we have to work, plan, and fight if we want to experience joy, love, adventure, and most of the good things in life. Every day, a beautiful sunset, a breathtaking waterfall, a moving book, and a best friend are out there for us to find; all are waiting outside your door. Hardship, like gravity, weighs us all down; the greatest joys only come to those who have the courage to fight for them, the tenacity to work for them, and the optimism to believe in them.

An optimist believes that no matter how bad things get, something amazingly good is right over the next mountain. From the worst of times, we can gain the wisdom and insights needed to experience the best of times. Optimists move through life with a certain energy, excitement, and enthusiasm not found in others. However, optimists are not delusional; they're realists. They understand that bad things are inevitable, so they prepare for tough times whenever possible, experience them honestly, learn from them, and move on.

For peak performers, optimism is a technique for seeing problems and obstacles as opportunities for growth, training, and wisdom. They operate with the belief that regardless of how bad things get, they have the ability to return their lives to a place of joy. Adopting this belief system yourself can actually create the energy and resources needed to address the problem at hand. In addition, taking this point of view will move you more rapidly from extreme discomfort to a more positive frame of mind.

Think about how optimism can help you in a physical fight. Close-quarter combat students are trained to cultivate a warrior's perspective. If a warrior ever finds himself lying under a barstool with a drunk, two-hundred-pound jerk's boot on his chest, the optimist's perspective is, "I've got him right where I want him." In this same situation, an untrained person would most likely be thinking, "God, why me?" Using an optimistic viewpoint doesn't change your reality—you're still down there on the floor—but training yourself to believe that you're in a good position frees the mind to continue searching for a solution, whereas thinking, "God, why me?" allows for nothing but self-pity and defeat.

The optimist sees the situation clearly, experiences the good and the bad aspects of it honestly, and then looks for options, lessons, and opportunities. In case you're wondering, there is a solution to the boot-on-the-chest problem, but I'd have to show you the moves in person.

WHEN ONE DOOR CLOSES, ANOTHER DOOR OPENS; BUT WE SO OFTEN LOOK SO LONG AND SO REGRETFULLY UPON THE CLOSED DOOR, THAT WE DO NOT SEE THE ONES WHICH OPEN FOR US.

ALEXANDER GRAHAM BELL

Growing Optimism

Your brain will seek out answers to the questions you ask it consistently. If you believe you are a victim, you are constantly asking, "Why me?" Your brain will tell you. This question has a lot of answers, and your brain will explain why you are fat, sad, broke, or in a bad relationship in great detail. If you've got a victim's brain, you'll hear about how much everyone else is at fault. I'm sure you've heard it yourself from someone else. Sit next to any victim at a dinner party, and you'll get a lot of reasons that his or her life isn't working. Sit next to an optimist, on the other hand, and you'll hear about how things will work out for the best. You'll also hear this optimist take responsibility for his or her situation, embrace its reality, and work on solutions—because an optimist's brain is answering the question, "How do I handle this?" instead of, "Why me?" The first step in growing optimism, therefore, is learning how to ask better questions. The act of goal setting covered in the goals chapter is a fine example of how optimism helps your brain find practical solutions. When you set goals, your brain is already working on a way to achieve them as soon as you write them down. Once you do that, you'll be far too busy pursuing and enjoying the things in life that matter to have time for pessimism.

Let me give you one warning about endless optimism. For the first thirty years of my life, I was really good at living the optimist creed, "When life gives you lemons, make lemonade." When confronted by any hardship, I would immediately try to find the good in the situation. What was the lesson in this for me? How could this make me a better person? I was great at answering these questions, but on some level, I knew I was missing an important step.

Then I figured it out. I got smacked in the face with the answer on the morning of the Oklahoma City bombings. I was attending a workshop in Los Angeles, and on hearing the news, I began searching for the lesson our society needed to learn from this tragedy. How could we prevent this from ever happening again? What had we done that would drive someone to do this? My thoughts were interrupted by a woman who asked the seminar facilitators if we could break and form a circle to pray for the families whose lives had been destroyed by this senseless act. She was visibly distraught, and as we held hands I could see the grief and pain she was experiencing, but I didn't feel a thing. I could find answers, but I couldn't feel any pain—I had gotten too good at making lemonade. As the group prayed for the families and victims, I remember praying as hard as I ever had, "Please, God, let me learn to feel. Let me be more than just happy." It took a lot of extraordinary events, both good and bad, but my prayers were answered.

To be truly human, we need to learn to experience and grow from the entire range of emotions. Ecstasy cannot truly be appreciated and understood without experiencing agony. The true beauty of life's symphony comes from the full range of our capacity to feel. There are no emotions that, when honestly experienced and honored, aren't part of our song. My sweetest moments have always come following my greatest struggles.

When life gives you lemons, it makes sense to taste how sour they are. Sorrow, anger, and rage are all appropriate and necessary emotions. The more honestly they are experienced, the more naturally they will leave your body. Many people believe that when we stifle these emotions, they come back to haunt us. Cancer, high blood pressure, heart attacks, and strokes can all be symptoms of bottled-up emotions. Yet, we shouldn't become dysfunctional when life's slings and arrows strike us. To feel an emotion honestly is not the same as acting on it. Rage can be directed into exercise, a punching bag, or a journal; unfortunately, it can also be directed at another human. Wisdom can guide us to the best use of these emotions, but whatever you do, please allow yourself time to grieve, cry, morn, and rage as you experience the inevitable pain in life. I had a good friend who, within a month of losing a parent, asked me if I thought she should be on medication because she felt she was struggling with depression. I told her, "You're not depressed—you're sad. You're supposed to be sad. Let it happen." What kind of society have we become if we aren't allowed to be sad? Who would say to this woman, "The funeral is over, come on, get over it"?

Step back from our world of instant gratification and allow your emotions to take the time they need. One of the beauties of spending time in nature is that you feel more connected to the natural cycles of life and death. Once you have taken the time to feel the sting of the lemons' acid, then you can begin to make lemonade by learning from the experience. Optimists look for the lessons to be learned from loss, challenge, and struggle. What has happened to us happens to all humans, as we move through the cycles of life. Death and loss allow us to appreciate the beauty of a sunset, the power of human touch, and the grace found in quiet.
You will be just fine!

WHAT SEEMS TO US AS BITTER TRIALS ARE OFTEN BLESSINGS IN DISGUISE.

OSCAR WILDE

Optimism Exercises

EXERCISE 1.
Take a moment and reflect on one of the more challenging times in your life.

_____
_____
_____
_____
_____
_____
_____

EXERCISE 2.
How has that challenge strengthened and empowered you? How has this event enabled you to have a richer life experience?

_____
_____
_____
_____
_____

EXERCISE 3.
When you are struck by tragedy or hardship, remember to breathe. For as long as we have breath, we have thoughts. And as long as we have thoughts, we have the ability to move our lives forward. Remember, where you are is exactly where you need to be. From this place you can launch yourself into an even greater place of joy and happiness and possibility! If you're reading this, then you have more than enough.

Gettysburg Address

Fourscore and seven years ago our fathers brought forth on this continent a new nation, conceived in liberty and dedicated to the proposition that all men are created equal.

Now we are engaged in a great civil war, testing whether that nation or any nation so conceived and so dedicated can long endure. We are met on a great battlefield of that war. We have come to dedicate a portion of that field as a final resting-place for those who here gave their lives that that nation might live. It is altogether fitting and proper that we should do this.

But in a larger sense, we cannot dedicate, we cannot consecrate, we cannot hallow this ground. The brave men, living and dead who struggled here have consecrated it far above our poor power to add or detract. The world will little note nor long remember what we say here, but it can never forget what they did here. It is for us the living rather to be dedicated here to the unfinished work which they who fought here have thus far so nobly advanced. It is rather for us to be here dedicated to the great task remaining before us—that from these honored dead we take increased devotion to that cause for which they gave the last full measure of devotion—that we here highly resolve that these dead shall not have died in vain, that this nation under God shall have a new birth of freedom, and that government of the people, by the people, for the people shall not perish from the earth.

ABRAHAM LINCOLN

P

<u>PERSEVERANCE</u>

The ability to achieve your goals by sticking to the task.

Perseverance won't guarantee success,
but quitting always guarantees failure!

WHEN THOMAS EDISON was asked by a reporter how he created the incandescent light bulb, Mr. Edison responded with a truth that should resonate with all of us. He said that after countless failed attempts, he simply ran out of new ways to fail, leaving success as his only option.

At my parents' fiftieth wedding anniversary, a friend of mine asked my dad how they were able to stay married for so long. My father smiled at my friend and said, "We never got divorced!"

I once asked the Grandmaster of an ancient martial arts tradition how he became head of his organization. His response, "I out-lived everyone else."

In each case, what led to a great achievement was simple: never give up! Gravity is a fact of life, and we work against it with our first breath. By fighting it, by persevering, we learn, against all odds, to stand, run, jump, and do a thousand other things with these gangly bodies of ours. Despite our earth-bound natures, we have soared with eagles in airplanes and become the first creatures to walk on the moon. To those who never give up, all things are possible.

There are a few principles universal to the achievement of great success; perseverance is one of them. More records, more world championships, and more miracles have taken place because of perseverance than because of any other single factor. Look through history, and you will discover that it far outweighs talent, intellect, education, or any other quality as the single attribute shared by most great achievers.

If great achievement were a treasure, then failure, disappointment, rejection, and boredom would be its guards. The average person can only encounter these foes so many times before he throws up his hands, packs his bags, and goes home. The exceptional man or woman counters failure with learning, disappointment with renewed hope, rejection with unwavering self-confidence, and boredom with a relentless passion toward the achievement of his or her goal. These rare men and women will meet their foes as often as needed, until the enemies, not themselves, are worn down! When these guards have sent home those lacking enough perseverance, the gates shall open and the true of heart shall be granted their treasure.

Also, never pick a fight with someone who doesn't know when to quit.

Perseverance at Work

Live long enough and you will discover the gift behind any great achievement is in the doing—and this is an important thing to remember. I would never counsel myself or others to pursue something that wasn't worth the effort—life is too short, and perseverance of an unworthy goal is a waste of time. When you are engaged in a labor of love, you can access the energy, knowledge, and people you need to accomplish your goal. Ask those who have accomplished great things if they had any regrets; the most frequent answer will be that their focus on the goal precluded them from enjoying the process. Success is ultimately the pursuit of a worthwhile goal—make sure all your goals meet this standard.

The perseverance required for the achievement of any goal is directly proportional to how big a bite you want to take out of life. If your goal is to climb Mount Whitney and you are reasonably healthy, you need somewhere between two to six months of training and a couple hundred bucks. If you intend to climb Mount Everest, you need years and years of training and hundreds of thousands of dollars. Both are totally achievable; one will just require a much larger perseverance muscle than the other.

Because life is short, we tend to have a very narrow perspective on things. If we don't get what we want, if we are rejected, or if we fail a few times, then we believe the goal is impossible or only reserved for someone else. The more global your perspective, the easier it will be to handle perceived failure, disappointment, and rejection. If you understand the value of resilience, you will find it much easier to get up, dust yourself off, and try again, knowing you have another hundred knockdowns to survive, before it's your turn to win.

Once you have fully committed yourself to a goal, the universe has a way of providing you with the training and experience you need to achieve it. However, this training often looks and feels like nothing you would have imagined. In hindsight, these seemingly random experiences will turn out to be a remarkably straight path toward your goal—but not while you're in the middle of them.

I even think we can see this principle at work in history, not only in our own lives. I am a huge fan of history and an even bigger fan of this great country of ours. For years, many historians have focused on America's shortcomings. At times, it almost seems as if people want the United States to apologize for actions now long in the past. I take the opposite approach. Like any entity comprised of humans, we have faults, but if you know your history, you understand that no other nation has ever provided its people with greater access to freedom and opportunity than the United States. You also understand there has never been another nation more willing to come to the aid of other countries in need. I believe that without America, the world would be a much darker place. Without the perseverance of one American president, we would be living a in a much less free and less humane world. No discussion of perseverance would be complete without sharing a bit of his story. Few historians will argue about the role Lincoln held in keeping our Union together during our country's worst crisis. What kind of training did our sixteenth President, Abraham Lincoln, receive that prepared him for such a momentous task?

The training he received was years and years of failure and rejection. Here's a short list—there actually are several more—of the life challenges of Abraham Lincoln:

He failed in business in 1831.
He was defeated for state legislator in '32.
He tried another business in '33. It failed.
His fiancée died in '35.
He had a nervous breakdown in '36.
In '43 he ran for Congress and was defeated.
He tried again in '48 and was defeated again.
He tried running for the Senate in '55. He lost.
The next year he ran for Vice President and lost.
In '59 he ran for the Senate again and was defeated.
In 1860 he was elected the 16th President of the United States.

This list is fairly well known, but it's all true—and he never gave up. Now how many auditions, job interviews, first dates, cold calls, knockdowns, and rejections can you handle?

You should also keep in mind that perseverance doesn't mean running into a brick wall until your head breaks. It means any time you run into a brick wall, you should look for whatever tools, information, or access you need to get over, around, or through it. Let others slam their heads into the wall, while you go in search of a ladder, a shovel, someone to boost you over, or some dynamite to blow the damn wall to bits.

Ask the stone smith who strikes the stone five hundred times with his hammer; is it the first, fiftieth, or five-hundredth strike that breaks the stone? Their answer will be yes. The fifty year marriage is created one day at a time; Mt. Everest is climbed one step at a time. The best thing about perseverance is its simplicity—all you do is keep going.

> OUR GREATEST GLORY IS NOT IN NEVER FALLING,
> BUT IN RISING EVERY TIME WE FALL.
>
> RALPH WALDO EMERSON

Growing Perseverance

Man has the capacity to learn, grow, and change (except for married men, but that's a subject for another day). Just as we can master a new language or sport, we have the ability to develop and master character traits. We see this every day in successful parenting, and it's the basis for any personal development program. To develop character traits, we study, observe, model, practice, review, and practice some more. The Chinese proverb, "He who has mastered one thing, has mastered all things," simply means that the techniques employed to excel at any aspect of life are transferable to other fields.

Growing perseverance is no different than improving your serve in tennis or taking a cooking class—work at one thing, and it will help the others. Here's what you need to do:

- Make it a goal: "I will develop and improve my ability to persevere!"
- Begin by making and honoring commitments to yourself.
- Start with small, achievable commitments and then add to them. For example: "I will make it to the gym twice a week for the next four weeks, no matter what." Next month, make it three times a week.
- As you complete each commitment, make the next one slightly more challenging.
- Read books and biographies about great achievers; all are filled with inspiring stories of perseverance in action.
- Remove *quit* from your vocabulary, replace the word *failure* with *setback*.
- Surround yourself with as many people as possible who support your goal.
- Celebrate your small successes along the way—everybody loves a celebration!
- Understand there is nothing perfect about you, this world, or your plan. Be prepared to make mistakes, screw up, fall down, look stupid, and get rejected. It won't kill you, and if it does, you're dead, so you won't have to worry about persevering any more.
- Every perceived failure takes you one step closer to success. In addition to being the home-run king, Babe Ruth held another record— more strike-outs than any other major league player!

The current divorce, obesity, college dropout, and business failure rates are testaments to how weak our nation's perseverance muscle has become. In my parents' generation, the mantra was "when the going gets tough, the tough get going." It appears that in today's feel-good, pop-psychology culture the mantra has become "when the going gets tough, quit and get someone else to do it for you."

When do we start teaching and practicing perseverance? The answer is *today*. Our children need to develop grit, and we need to show them how. We grow perseverance in our children the same way we develop it in ourselves, by following through, keeping commitments, and not quitting. When you sign your three- to four-year-old child up for a class, make sure you keep the time commitment short: a maximum of two to twelve weeks. Discuss the importance of developing their perseverance muscle, and let them know that you really want them to have fun. But once they start the class, they will finish it, no matter what. When the class is over, make a big deal about what your child has accomplished, find out what he or she liked and disliked, and guide your child to their next commitment. I remember a single mom of a four-year-old boy calling me one day at the karate studio. She said she couldn't get Timmy to come to class. I asked how big Timmy was. There was silence on the other end of the line, but she got my point! After all, God made our children smaller than we are for a reason. If our children can learn to play video games, they are old enough to start developing perseverance.

Overcoming the Enemies

The four enemies of perseverance are failure, disappointment, rejection, and boredom. Here are the steps to help you overcome each of these enemies:

FAILURE.

+ **Recognize each failed attempt for what it is—an opportunity to gain feedback.** What skills did you lack, what preparation was incomplete, or what new information do you need for your next attempt? Find out, and use that information to your benefit.
+ **Keep in mind that you can try unsuccessfully thousands of times and not be a failure.** You only fail when you quit! How many times did you fall while learning to walk or to ride a bike?

DISAPPOINTMENT.

+ **Remember, disappointment only occurs when the outcome doesn't meet our expectation.** You are in control of your preparation and your expectations; you are not always in control of the outcome. Expect the best, be prepared for the worst.
+ **Expect to learn, do your best, and enjoy the process.** By modifying your expectations, you can defeat disappointment while still moving closer to your goal.
+ **Keep in mind that if you are succeeding 100 percent of the time, you are aiming too low!** If you are not challenged by your goals, you're wasting your time.

REJECTION.

+ Don't forget, rejection is only evidence that you haven't presented your-self, your product, or your idea as effectively as you need to do. Either that, or you have made your presentation to the wrong person. Focus on your market, continue working on your presentation, and do it again.
+ Remember, the rejection of an idea, proposal, or a piece of your work, is not a rejection of you! Develop enough confidence in your-self to be bigger than any one thing that could be rejected.
+ Never forget, great men and women want you to succeed, the small and weak want you to fail! Don't let anyone get you down, and look for encouragement from good people.

BOREDOM.

+ Success requires proficiency; proficiency requires perfection of the basics; perfecting the basics is boring, so just deal with it! Seriously, it's your goal, not mine, and if it's important enough to you, then you will do all of the necessary ground work to succeed.
+ Life masters realize it's impossible to do the same thing twice, so they find the newness in every practice session. In every practice, the timing, the energy, and our skills will never be exactly the same. Life masters look upon each repetition as a new moment and enjoy the tiny discoveries to be found in them.
+ Don't be afraid to take a break if you have lost your creative juice, step away for a time—it will be there when you get back. Perseverance is a skill to be employed in the pursuit of things that matter—adjust your goals when you find what matters to you has changed.

PERSEVERANCE IS NOT A LONG RACE;
IT IS MANY SHORT RACES ONE AFTER ANOTHER.

WALTER ELLIOTT

Perseverance Exercises

EXERCISE 1.

Write down a time in your past when you felt defeated. Who were the key players, and what were the key events?

_____
_____
_____
_____
_____

Now with the power of distance and 20/20 hindsight, list at least three life-altering benefits that came about as a result of that perceived failure!

1._____
2._____
3._____

EXERCISE 2.

The next time you feel like things are coming apart, review the gifts and lessons learned from other life challenges, and keep your eyes open for the lessons and opportunities to be found in this current struggle!

Keep a-Goin'

Ef you strike a thorn or rose,
Keep a-goin'!
Ef it hails or if it snows,
Keep a-goin'!

'Taint no use to sit an' whine
When the fish ain't on your line;
Bait your hook an' keep a-tryin'—
Keep a-goin'!

When the weather kills your crop,
Keep a-goin'!
Though 'tis work to reach the top,
Keep a-goin'!

S'pose you're out o' ev'ry dime,
Gittin' broke ain't any crime;
Tell the world you're feelin' prime—
Keep a-goin'!

When it looks like all is up,
Keep a-goin'!
Drain the sweetness from the cup,
Keep a-goin'!

See the wild birds on the wing,
Hear the bells that sweetly ring,
When you feel like sighin', sing—
Keep a-goin'!

FRANK LEBBY STANTON

Q
QUALITY

Self-definition through every thought, word, and deed.

THE BEST WAY TO GUARANTEE LOYALTY FROM YOUR FAMILY MEMBERS, FRIENDS, TEAMS, AND CLIENTS IS TO PERFORM. THE QUALITY OF OUR ACTIONS ROARS ABOVE THE BEAUTY OF OUR WORDS.

WE WERE FLYING at 7,000 feet out of Palm Springs, on our way home from a perfect getaway weekend. I had received my pilot's license only a few weeks before, and I had always wanted to take a trip like this one. It was 1991; my wife was six-months pregnant, and for her, going on a flight with me at the controls was a huge leap of faith. We had been on a few sightseeing flights before, but this was our first real adventure. I had logged about a hundred hours of flying time by then, and that tends to be a dangerous time for a new pilot—everything has been fine so far, so sometimes a pilot can get cocky.

This flight looked and felt easy. I could see forever, and I had the plane trimmed for the best climb. We had gotten above a little bit of turbulence near Banning Pass, a place outside Palm Springs with a big field of windmills. I was looking down at them when I felt a sudden drop in engine power. I immediately looked at the instruments. I saw that our engine was growing progressively weaker, its revolutions heading downward in spurts. I watched the tachometer dropping and rising, dropping and rising, with each rise a little lower, until suddenly there was a frightening silence. My engine was dead, and now our lives depended on how quickly I could become a glider pilot.

Things looked bad, but I had something good on my side: trust. My wife trusted me; I trusted my training; my training led me to the right actions and decisions. That's when you understand the value of "perfect practice," when you put your best effort into training, so that you'll be ready when the real thing happens. As a close-quarter combat instructor, I had made quality training into more than an expression—it was the difference between life and death. Here, we were looking at the same critical choices. My wife asked what she should do, and I said, in the annoyingly calm voice all good pilots cultivate, "Breathe, and reach behind my seat for the flight manual." Now it was my turn to breathe. That's the first rule of behavior when you find yourself in a dangerous situation: slow down and move with precision. Then I went down the list of procedures for this situation: first, trim the plane for best glide speed (fortunately, small airplanes really are good gliders), then, notify air traffic control. By then, I had over 7,000 feet of altitude to try for a restart or find a place to land. I checked the instruments again; my glide speed was perfect. I looked around—I saw no other traffic and I had good visibility—so I tried to restart the engine: nothing. Now we were at 6,200 feet. I checked the instruments again: my air speed was good, well above the velocity that would cause the airplane to stall. I took a quick look at the flight map, and found that Banning airport was within our glide range. By the time we had dropped to 5,500 feet, the airport was in view off our left wing, about three-quarters of a mile away. I checked the instruments again and took another visual traffic scan; everything was still OK. Air traffic control gave me the radio frequency for Banning. I went on the air and set the radio. When we passed through 4,000 feet, I made a last attempt to restart the engine: again, nothing.

At that point, we were committed to a no-power landing. As we flew directly over the airport, I announced our intention to land over the open frequency, so that everyone in the vicinity with an aviation radio would know what was going on. As we passed through 2,500 feet, I got ready to land. The key to a no-power landing, I recalled, is to fly the pattern a little high and tight, to make sure you don't land short or overshoot. I trimmed for the best approach speed and made gentle turns, because the plane would hit the ground hard and kill us all if I stalled. I breathed and completed the base leg of the approach pattern, checked the instruments again, and turned onto the final approach. I knew that without power, I couldn't go around and try again—there was only one chance to do this right. I saw that I was coming in a little high, but my airspeed was good. I got the runway numbers from air traffic control, and then put out the flaps to lower our altitude a bit. Now we were at 600 feet, with our wings level and, thank God, no wind to knock the plane around. We floated downward until we felt the air pushing back off the ground (it's called *ground effect*). Then the wheels touched down—no bounce at all—it was my best landing ever! After we rolled to a stop, they towed the plane to the shop while I went calmly into the men's room, closed the stall door, and dropped to my knees overcome by nausea, gratitude, tears, and emotion.

Over the next couple of years, I logged hundreds of hours of flight time without further incident, but I never lost the edge I gained in that experience. Today, as I look into the eyes of Robin and my three girls, I will be forever grateful to my instructors who taught me to only accept perfect practice.

Accept nothing but the highest quality performance in practice, and you'll be ready when the real thing arrives.

Quality at Work

Quality has been at the center of this book since the beginning. Its purpose is to give you a combination of personal challenges and tools that will help you achieve a life of greater significance and joy. I created it with the hope of inspiring, nagging, and motivating you to improve the quality of each day you have on this planet.

I didn't understand the importance of quality until I began studying close-quarter combat. In most things, we have a long lag time between the actions we choose and their consequences—but that's not true of close-quarter combat. Teenagers can take their education for granted and, other than suffering the pain of complaining parents, feel no consequences for almost a decade. By the time they experience the pain of doing nothing or, at best, having a crummy job, their lifestyles are so entrenched that it would take a super-human effort to change them! In a knife fight, the lag time between action and consequence is non-existent—and this truth accelerates the learning curve faster than anything else I have ever seen. With instant, accurate feedback, we make different choices, test them, and learn to get the results we seek consistently. In addition, honest combat training is effective because the consequences of failure are great. If you fail a test in school, you get a piece of paper, and maybe you feel a little bad about it. If you fail a knife fight, your friends and family feel very bad because you're dead.

If we could only look at our lives as survival situations (which, by the way, they are), we would be much more motivated to make better choices and commit to a higher level of quality. If I could show any teenage smoker how he'll look when he's dying from black lung years later, he'd become a nonsmoker on the spot. If I could show a new exercise client lacking energy, self-esteem, and a love-life what it would be like to have the vitality, confidence, and enjoyment she'd deserve, I could show you a life-long fitness fanatic. Creating quality is all about connecting actions to consequences.

The contrary principle is also true—poor performance occurs when we fail to sense that our actions are directly connected to their outcomes. If the person on the assembly line assembling the rocket engine doesn't understand the significance of a rubber gasket to the mission's success or failure, then you get a Columbia Space Shuttle disaster. If you can connect each action to its ultimate impact on your life, you will make better choices. Make this connection, and you will no longer accept mediocrity from your education, your relationships, your body, or yourself.

I have always believed that we are children of God and that excellence is not just our birthright, but also our sacred charge. Why should we fail to achieve greatness when we have everything we need to do it? Who are we to fail to live up to that standard when God has provided so much? The quality of your life will be defined by the quality of every thought, word, and deed you manifest on a daily basis—so go out there and do it! A lack of potential is no crime; not living up to our potential is a shame. Live up to yours!

NOTHING DOESN'T MATTER.

HATSUMI SENSEI

Growing Quality

Growing quality is much easier than you might think; it begins simply with a sincere commitment to making tiny, consistent, incremental improvements in what you are currently doing. A common mistake people make is putting too much pressure on themselves and expecting too much change, too quickly. As critical as weight lifting is to your overall health and fitness, nothing will get you out of the gym faster than an injury caused by too much weight, too soon. You can also see people doing too much, too soon in what I call "New Year Syndrome." We spend a lifetime screwing up aspects of our lives, January 1st comes along, and we expect to change everything overnight. When the results we want don't come back instantly, we get frustrated and fall back into the habits that created the mess in the first place.

When I speak of tiny, consistent, incremental improvements, what I mean specifically is about 2 percent a week. That's what I use for myself and my clients, and I mean that literally: a measurable 2 percent improvement. I have found this to be a totally unintimidating and completely achievable objective that, over time, will always result in a goal achieved with a relatively small investment in time and energy. Imagine this kind of yearly improvement to your body, your relationships, your home, and your finances. No one has embraced this concept better than the Japanese manufacturing sector. As a kid growing up in the sixties, "Made in Japan" was synonymous with "cheap, badly made stuff." Today, Japanese companies have become the gold standard for quality in cars, electronics, and even pianos, along with many other things, leaving many American manufacturers struggling for survival.

I am also a huge believer in modeling and immersion as ways to grow quality. Modeling is the technique of finding someone who represents the best-in-class in your desired area, studying him, and adopting his practices. It's simple; do what the best-in-class do long enough, and you will become like one of them! Immersion follows a similar principle. Immerse yourself in high-quality surroundings—find a place full of people who strive to be their best. Their energy will drive you to even higher levels of performance. It's even the same with objects. You don't need to own much of anything, but learn to look for quality in the things you purchase and use. You may come to learn that the products of the highest function and quality are not always the most expensive.

Ultimately, quality is about becoming the kind of person others can depend on. If you run a business well, people trust you and are comfortable referring their family and friends to you. Few satisfactions are greater than being recognized as someone who provides high-quality products and services. Life is far too short to be known for anything less.

THEY WILL RISE HIGHEST WHO STRIVE FOR THE HIGHEST PLACES.

LATIN PROVERB

Quality Exercises

EXERCISE 1.
Select one area of your life currently suffering from mediocrity. For the next month, commit to a 2 percent weekly improvement in the performance quality of this activity. This exercise will require some thought on your part. This improvement could be as simple as increasing the weight plate on each exercise at the gym or cutting sodas from your diet. It may be something more complex, requiring some coaching, a lesson, or getting access to a new tool or technique. Find it, measure it, and do it!

EXERCISE 2.
Model the best practice in this area. Search websites, schools, and personal contacts for access to someone who does this activity better than you do. Add at least one best-practice technique to what you are currently doing.

EXERCISE 3.
Make quality a focus in your daily life. Print the word *Quality* and put it on your fridge; start each day's journal or calendar with it. Practice it at every opportunity. You can exercise your quality muscle by how you make a bed, weed a garden, or cook dinner.

EXERCISE 4.
Many people are speeding down the "it's not so bad" superhighway moving faster and faster to their ultimate destination—death. Peak performers find satisfaction and joy in a job well done. It was one of "the greatest generations" mantras: "If a job is worth doing, it's worth doing well." It would serve you well to adopt it! Learn to take pride in a job well done. Think of each and every action you take as your signature to the world.

By A Person Of Quality

Remote from Strife, from urban Throngs, and Noise.
Here dwells my Soul amidst domestic Joys:
No ratling Coaches serious Thoughts annoy;
Nor busy prating Fools my Peace destroy:
Wrapt up in all the Sweets of rural Ease,
My great Creator's Works my Senses please.
The Mind, in peaceful Solitude, has Room
To range in Thought, and ramble far from home,
Others may court the Joys which Princes give,
Whilst I, in sacred Silence, truly live.

MARY BARBER

R
<u>RESPONSIBILITY</u>

1. The physical, mental, and emotional ability to respond to any given challenge. 2. The extent to which you consider caring for your life, your family, your community, and your world to be your job!

YOU ARE THE ONLY ONE WHO HOLDS THE RESPONSIBILITY FOR CREATING THE WORLD YOU WANT TO LIVE IN AND THE LIFE YOU WANT TO LEAD.

Few things can launch me onto my soap box faster than seeing someone failing to accept responsibility for his or her actions and their consequences. The other day I happened to see the cover story of a gossip magazine. The latest Hollywood drama queen was kneeling on the cover in a bright pink bikini, and the headline over her in a giant, bold font read, "The Hills Made Me Bulimic." I could feel the veins throbbing in my neck, as the blood ran up into my brain and nearly made my head explode.

No my dearest, young empty-headed starlet, the Hills, Hollywood, your boyfriend, your mom, and President Obama didn't make you bulimic—your own act of shoving your finger down your throat after binging made you bulimic! At this point, I'm sure some of you are thinking, "OK, that's a little too harsh." On the contrary—I'm not being harsh enough. When I look at all of the troubles facing our world today, I can find none more devastating than our cultural loss of personal responsibility.

When did it become someone else's responsibility to feed, clothe, educate, entertain, dictate, and lord over me from birth until the day I die? America's Founding Fathers argued for our right to life, liberty, and the pursuit of happiness—they didn't guarantee happiness, or anything else! They had the wisdom to understand that life is fragile, impermanent, and fraught with hardship. They also knew that the greatest happiness only comes when we have pursued it ourselves. The beauty of this great human adventure is our unique, creative, and personal power. When we turn over responsibility for any aspect of our life to another person, organization, church, political party, or guru, we hand over equal parts of our potential for dignity and self-mastery. As Shakespeare wisely said, "The fault, dear Brutus, is not in the stars, but in ourselves."

Responsibility at Work

Your personal power is directly linked to your ability to respond to any given challenge or opportunity. What you can do in any situation grows or shrinks in relation the amount of responsibility you take for your life and the world around you.

Let me give you some examples from both extremes of the spectrum of responsibility. Infants have very little ability to respond to anything; therefore, they are totally dependent upon us for their survival. The ability of Navy Seals to respond is enormous; therefore, they are frequently called upon to solve an extraordinary range of problems all over the world. Where you and I fit on this spectrum is determined by how consistent and effective our training has been and the amount of responsibility we take for the outcomes we create. For that reason, we should make a life-long effort to expand our ability to respond, and with it, make a daily effort to expand the amount of responsibility we take for our lives.

The challenges and opportunities you face in this lifetime can only be met by your physical, mental, emotional, and spiritual tools. Your success or failure is determined by how well you apply these tools to each challenge or opportunity. A well-trained, extremely fit mountain climber has a high probability of success when he attempts to reach the summit of Mount Everest. His ability to respond to anything that happens on the mountain is extremely high; weather permitting, he should succeed. An intelligent, well-educated, and healthy CEO should be able to direct and manage the turnaround of an ailing company. Again, the tools this woman takes into the boardroom are her own to develop and use for the ultimate success of her company.

In close-quarter combat training, warriors learn that knives and guns are not weapons, but simply tools. The warrior himself is the weapon. We lose power when we fail to take responsibility for our actions and attempt to transfer that responsibility to objects. Sometimes I give a particular demonstration when I speak at elementary schools. I gather the children around a table and lay out several props: a Bible, some money, a set of car keys, a bottle of wine, a light socket (to represent electricity), and a training (non-functional) hand gun. Then I have them play the good/ bad game. I hold my hand over each item and ask them to tell me whether each item is good or bad. This is how it usually goes: When my hand is over the Bible, I hear "GOOD!" Over the money, "GOOD!" Over the car keys, "GOOD!" Over the wine, "BAD!" Over the light socket, "GOOD! Over the gun, "BAD!" These kids always show total conviction and feel great about being right. While they're still glowing from their success, I start asking them some questions. I go back to the Bible and ask them, "If the Bible told you to be kind to others, is that good?" That always gets a big, "YES"—but then I ask, "What if the Bible told you to hurt a woman because she was divorced, would that be good?" They start to look a little puzzled at this point, but I keep asking questions. "What if I use my money to pay someone to hurt another person?" "What if my mom and dad celebrate the birth of my sister with a glass of champagne?" "What if a police officer uses his gun to protect my family?"

No, I'm not trying to be mean, and they all get the point pretty quickly, as you should. Each item is extremely powerful, but power in itself is neither good nor bad. Power is good or bad when applied to a situation. When we demonize an object, all we are doing is disempowering people. The blame, the opportunity, and most importantly, the responsibility do not lie with the object but with the user. In 1930, if you asked a class of American first graders whether a gun was good or bad, they would most likely have told you, "GOOD!" If you ask the same question to first graders today, you would probably hear the opposite answer. Guns haven't changed much in eighty years, but attitudes toward them have. Their power lies only in their application—and for that, we must take responsibility. My point to them—and to you—is that we should learn how to think about objects and situations, so we can make our own decisions and be responsible for them. When we begin telling students what to think, instead of how to think, all we're doing is taking responsibility away from them, instead of teaching them to take it upon themselves.

Now that we've had a look at the tools you use for responsibility, it's time to look at the other half of the equation: responsibility for others. If I were the smartest, strongest, most loving person in the world, but all I did was live in a cave alone, what value would I be to myself or anyone else? History's most powerful men and women have always been those who accepted the greatest amount of responsibility for their lives and the world around them. Mother Teresa's power stemmed from the belief that it was her responsibility to care for God's weak, sick, and needy. She didn't wait for someone else to fix the poverty and disease she saw around her; she got to work fixing it, and in doing so, made the world a much brighter place. All great causes and global changes have been driven by men and women unwilling to leave the work to someone else.

If this sounds too idealistic for you, consider the opposite attitude: leaving the responsibility to others. It's easy to do when you think every problem is someone else's fault. This belief allows us to spend our time complaining about our lives instead of taking up the much harder task of actually fixing things. Unfortunately, there are a number of reasons that this belief simply isn't true:

+ If everybody is waiting for someone else to fix things, nothing will ever get fixed.
+ Joy is found in creating for yourself and others, not taking from them.
+ My vision for your life will never be as beautiful as your own.
+ Blaming anyone for anything has never fixed it!
+ Without the skill sets developed by problem solving, someone might get you out of one problem, but ultimately, you'll get in more trouble somewhere else.

IN DREAMS BEGINS RESPONSIBILITY.

WILLIAM BUTLER YEATS

Growing Responsibility

The first step in growing your responsibility is to accept the fact that in the movie of your life, you are the star, the writer, and the director. No one will have a greater impact on what your life becomes than you. Whether it's comedy, romance, drama, or horror, your life is yours to create, rewrite, and experience as long as you are alive and willing. There will be many other actors in your story with varying levels of impact on you. Some are people you have invited, many are not. In the end, no one controls the way you respond, react, or create more than you do. Hero or villain, loved or hated, remembered or forgotten, each character you play is determined by the choices you make and how you think, speak, and act yourself in your glorious story. You might be thinking, "That sounds great, but what about the bad things that happen to me? I didn't create them or ask for them." No, but you have total control over how you respond to them. When John Walsh's child was abducted and murdered he had no control over the crime, but he was able to use his pain and rage to start the *America's Most Wanted* television show; as a result, hundreds of felons have been arrested and countless lives have been saved. So often in life, good or bad is a matter of perspective, and when we look back with the wisdom that time and distance bring us, we can often see how tragedy has moved us to take some amazing responsibility that we would never have considered in other circumstances.

Once you gain clarity as to your starring role, make a commitment to remove two words from your vocabulary: blame and excuse. Examine your life in its totality—your relationships, your education, your body, your career, all that you have created: the good, the bad, and the ugly. Accept it for what it is, without blame or excuse, and commit today to take full responsibility for improving the quality of any areas that need to be improved. It is no one else's job to make your life better; the responsibility does not belong to your parents, your spouse, your children, or your representative. No one has a better understanding of your needs, your desires, and your capabilities. No one else has a greater ability to improve the quality of your life than you can. No one else can fix, heal, love, create, grow, and repair the things that surround you better than you do.

A Russian proverb reminds us, "To change the world, begin with your front porch." If you see something in your life, your home, or your world that needs to be done, do it! Be clear about this: every pain you have, every dream you imagine, and every creation you make begins with your first breath and ends with your last. As I've said before, the more responsibility you take, the more power you have.

If it's all up to you, "you" had better be incredible, so remember to work on your ability-to-respond training. Throughout this book, we've worked consistently on a balanced approach to your training. Since the purpose of education is to increase your ability to respond to opportunities and challenges, then you should already be on your way to taking responsibility for your success and failures. Let's take another look at your ongoing educational process and review its strengths and weakness.

Using the best life you can imagine as the model, we're going to look at each of life's main components and grade them. If your health, energy, and body aren't what they could and should be, then stop waiting for the magic pill, stop covering your body in clothing and cars. Get access to the training and information you need to rebuild it the way it needs to be. If you want your relationship to be great, then make it so. If you want your health to be great, then make it so. If you want your world to be great, then make it so.

By the way, as effective as these universal truths and exercises may be, it's important to understand that I'm human too, and I need to take my own advice as much as anyone. Life is a constant struggle against our weaknesses and gravity. I can be in perfect physical shape today, but if I stop training, in a matter of weeks I will begin losing the physique that I have spent a lifetime creating. We are defined by our struggles, and I really mean "we." I promise you that I am standing right by your side struggling, just as you are.

ONE SHOULD SEE THE WORLD AND SEE HIMSELF AS A SCALE
WITH AN EQUAL BALANCE OF GOOD AND EVIL.
WHEN HE DOES ONE GOOD DEED, THE SCALE IS TIPPED TO THE GOOD—
HE AND THE WORLD IS SAVED. WHEN HE DOES ONE EVIL DEED, THE SCALE IS
TIPPED TO THE BAD—HE AND THE WORLD IS DESTROYED.

MAIMONIDES

Responsibility Exercises

EXERCISE 1.

In the following areas, grade yourself as being above your expectations, meeting your expectations, or needs improvement.

Education and knowledge_____

Self-confidence_____

Physical health, strength, and beauty_____

Spiritual strength_____

Grade the following relationships:

Significant other_____

Children_____

Parents_____

Friends_____

Community_____

Grade your performance in the following areas:

Business and career_____

Savings and investments_____

Play, travel, and recreation_____

Write in and grade three areas specific to your life vision:

_____

_____

_____

EXERCISE 2.

Select three areas that you scored as "needs improvement" where improvement would have the greatest positive impact on your life. Move them to the top of your to-do list for this month.

EXERCISE 3.

Create an action plan for each item, including the education, resources, and time needed to improve them.

EXERCISE 4.

Schedule them into your weekly calendar.

Peace Prayer of St. Francis

Lord, make me an instrument of your peace.
Where there is hatred, let me sow love.
Where there is injury, pardon.
Where there is doubt, faith.
Where there is despair, hope.
Where there is darkness, light.
Where there is sadness, joy.

O Divine Master,
grant that I may not so much seek
to be consoled, as to console;
to be understood, as to understand;
to be loved, as to love.
For it is in giving that we receive.
It is in pardoning that we are pardoned,
and it is in dying that we are born to Eternal Life.
Amen.

SAINT FRANCIS OF ASSISI

S
<u>SERVICE</u>

The path to our highest joy is found in taking loving action on behalf of our family, friends, community, and world.

The greatest demonstration of love and power occurs when we act outside of our immediate self-interest in the Service of others.

One beautiful fall afternoon, I took a sunset walk with my father and my daughter Becca. At the time, we represented the full range of ages—Becca was almost one; I was forty-seven; my dad was eighty-eight. I held hands with both of them, and I felt instability on both sides. Becca's little body was learning how to walk; the chemo treatments were making my dad's cancer-riddled body unsteady. Together, the three of us could only make it about two hundred yards, but that was enough to take us into the heart of a beautiful old oak forest and make the trip worthwhile. On our way home, my dad's shaky steps, aided by me and my father's cane, were a perfect match for my little girl's wobbly new gait. It was slow going, but I felt continuity and peace.

When we got back to the house, Robin took Becca, and it was time for my dad's bath. He never allowed the hospice nurses to bathe him; that responsibility fell to my brother and me. Over the years, I've heard horror stories about the humiliation, embarrassment, and anguish that go along with helping your parents die. The chemotherapy treatments that were supposed to extend his life almost killed him, and after spending a week in intensive care, the doctors finally sent him home to die with us. My brother and I, together with our families, took turns caring for him. Daily, we would do everything in our power to help him find reasons to live; and when the time came, we would help him leave this world with grace and dignity.

He was easy to lift into the tub now; the body that once belonged to "Handy Hal" was at least fifty pounds lighter. I'd made sure the water was the right temperature. I took him in my arms and carefully slid him from a specially designed chair into the bath. Once he was clean, he needed a shave. Sitting on the edge of the tub, I'd cover his face with lather and do my best not to cut him, which was much harder than you can imagine—it's actually very hard to shave someone else's face, rather than your own. He grumbled about the process, but we all knew how much better the baths made him feel. The problem wasn't the physical part—it was how much he hated his increasing dependence on his family. His mind stayed sharp until the end, but his body failed him, ultimately reaching a point where he needed us for everything. He would say he loved us more in the last three months of his life than I remember him saying in the previous forty-seven years, but almost every "I love you" was accompanied by "I'm so sorry that I'm such a pain." We tried to help him understand that doing things for the man who had done so much for all of his children was the privilege of a lifetime. I experienced more joy and growth serving the man who had raised me than I can say. For me, there was no sorrow in caring for him—the anguish would come two months later, when he died.

Service at Work

To understand service, we need to look deeply at the nature of humanity. Human beings have always been social animals; our relatively weak bodies and powerful intellects make forming a pack essential to our survival. Our greatest accomplishments are collective and cumulative, the result of the efforts of many people over many generations. Still, as much as we may appreciate these collective efforts, we tend to be most inspired by individual accomplishments. We are also, by our very nature, self-centered. To be a member of a pack, yet also self-centered, does not mean you hold inherently conflicting values, if you understand that your pack's welfare and your own are inseparable. By defining human beings as self-centered, I don't mean selfish; I am simply emphasizing the fact that we can only learn, see, experience, and touch the world around us from our own unique and deeply personal perspectives. We are literally the center of our universe; every experience we have is interpreted from our relatively small personal perspective. Since the goal of this manual is to help you create a bigger, brighter life, let's look at how a highly evolved, yet nevertheless self-centered, member of a pack would behave.

This enlightened being, through his or her deep connection to others, is driven towards a life of service. The surest path to personal joy and prosperity for this person involves empowering others. How does this process work? It comes from the understanding that what goes around, comes around. A healthy, self-centered person strives for a world filled with as much joy as possible by helping others find it. He or she realizes that it is impossible to hurt another person without hurting oneself. Any time we help make another person's life brighter, safer, happier, and more fulfilled, the same rewards reflect back on us. Therefore, service to another is the highest expression of self-love—it means truly living the Golden Rule. Although it may seem that pursuing selfish goals can lead to happiness, the opposite is actually the case. We find peace in nature, and joy when our relationships are in harmony, because on the most basic level we are intimately connected to everything. Clean air, fresh water, and nutritious food sustain our bodies; while love, companionship, and learning sustain our souls. As we grow and evolve, we feel our connection to others more readily; we experience more of each other's joy and sorrows, highs and lows.

The other morning, I read about a young California Highway Patrol officer who was killed riding his motorcycle home from work. The story included a picture of his young widow and their four-year-old daughter. Halfway through the story, my eyes were full of tears, my throat was tight, and I could feel my body responding in pain to this family's tragedy. We cry at weddings and funerals, get goose bumps watching the Olympics, and cheer for the underdog because we are all connected; we are members of the same family. This connection is what makes each of our journeys so beautiful and so painful. Truly evolved, self-centered people will work to make the world as bright and beautiful as they can. When we lay down our lives in service to others, we are ultimately acting in our own self-interest. Don't you want to be surrounded by happy, healthy, brilliant, loving people? Have you experienced any joy greater than when you have brought joy to others? What benefit is there to fame, glory, and riches if you have no one to share these rewards with? None at all—so become someone who gives to others: a leader, a servant, or both.

What do I mean by "both"? It's actually difficult to differentiate between a great servant and a great leader, and by the way, there is great honor in being a servant. In fact, when service or leadership is directed toward a greater good, the titles become interchangeable. Gandhi, Martin Luther King, George Patton, Abraham Lincoln, and Mother Teresa all devoted their lives in service of humanity; the world was made better by their efforts. Parents who sacrifice daily for their children, the volunteers at every great service organization, and countless others who understand the gift of service are all cut from the same cloth. They all are blessed with the knowledge that, by their service, their worlds are made brighter and more beautiful.

We all thrive when we devote ourselves to the service of others. Move through a typical day and think about how little you have actually contributed to your current life experience. Think about the objects that make up your daily life. From the alarm clock that starts your day, to the food that fills your kitchen, to the power that heats your home, to the modes of transportation you employ as you move through your life—how many of these items did you actually create yourself? We enjoy so much of what our world has to offer because of the service of others—and that means any act undertaken for the benefit of another. We may receive financial rewards for our professional services, but we also receive intrinsic and deeply personal rewards for what we provide our families, neighbors, and communities. We serve those groups because of the joy it brings us and the beauty it creates in our lives, rather than for the recognition or external rewards that might come our way. There are no medals or awards for the parents who change a diaper at three in the morning, but there ought to be. Parents are rarely recognized for the enormous amount of work they do—cleaning, cooking, washing clothes, or hauling the kids around town for school, sports practices, and music lessons. Few of those who volunteer at church or the local food kitchen, and few members of the PTA or all those booster clubs, can expect to appear on the cover of *People*. (To be fair, *People* does devote an occasional cover to an non-celebrity who has done something extraordinary, but that's the exception, rather than the rule.) That's fine, because we understand that the great joys in life come about from doing an important job well, not from the recognition it may bring. Who we become by doing the act is often much greater than the act itself. We serve because we are self-centered; we serve because it is healthy and appropriate to want happiness for our family. It is self-serving to strive to make our home and our neighborhood as safe and beautiful as possible. We serve because if we don't make our world better, no one will!

Think about those for whom service forms the greater part of their professional lives too. The financial rewards people receive for our professional services are generally in direct proportion to the perceived value they create. Fast food cook, retail clerk, or farm laborer—each of these servers does something for us that we don't have to do ourselves. The physician, the real estate agent, and the corporate executive are all engaged in acts of service to humanity. The physician heals us, the real-estate agent helps us find and purchase a home, and the executive, through proper employment of intellectual capital, creates jobs, products, services, and investment opportunities.

Our rewards for our services are tied directly to the amount of perceived value they create for others, but the key word here is "perceived." Why does the professional athlete or actor make millions, while the police officer and school teacher struggle to make ends meet? Although actors and athletes do provide us with a pleasant distraction that we find valuable, their rewards are large mainly because the number of people they reach is huge; millions of people are drawn to a hit movie or the playoffs. On the other hand, a teacher or police officer has the power to actually transform our lives. What value would you place on having the life of a family member saved, or being provided with the tools and education you need to make your dreams a reality? Unfortunately, even the best teachers and law enforcement officers only reach a relatively small number of people over the course of their careers. Fortunately, money is only one of the rewards that people can receive for their services. For them, the rewards are intrinsic. Only a teacher who has nurtured a young mind and spirit can describe the rewards associated with that tremendous service. Speak with a police officer who has had the privilege of returning a lost or kidnapped child to the parents, and you can see why many serve professionally for much more than a pay check.

If you love what you do and would like to experience greater financial abundance, look at ways to serve more people or find ways of changing people's perception about the value of your service. Great teachers have gone on to write great books, so instead of giving lectures heard only by hundreds, their writings are passed on to millions.

LIGHT IS THE TASK WHERE MANY SHARE THE TOIL.

HOMER

Growing Service

As I said before, service is any act undertaken for the benefit of others. Right now, I'd like to focus on the part that says "any act." It's easy to commit frequent daily acts of service, and they don't have to be huge. Growing service is really about growing your connection to the people and places around you. If someone drove by your house and threw trash on your lawn, would you leave it there? No! You wouldn't think of leaving trash on your lawn. Well, remember, if you're really self-centered, then should you leave trash lying on the ground in your park or in your child's schoolyard? If one of your neighbors were struggling to carry a heavy bag from their car, would you even think twice about going over and helping? Of course not—you'd immediately go over there and help. Well, how big is your neighborhood? It's as big as you can imagine, even if that means the entire world.

Is the world really yours? In a sense, we own nothing at all. At best, we serve as stewards of our bodies, our families, our communities, and the world we inhabit. My family is preparing for the two-hundredth anniversary of our stewardship of Rancho San Julian in 2016. I was raised to believe that it is each generation's duty to love, honor, and care for the ranch and pass it on to the next generation in even better condition than we found it. As highly evolved members of the human pack, I believe we should all look at our lives and worlds the same way. As stewards or servants of our body, family, community, and world, it is our moral obligation to take the best care of each of these as possible and to pass on something greater as a result of our efforts. This ideal is the principle of service.

Just as we love to serve, an important part of growing service is creating opportunities for others to serve. Remember, we are not here to dance alone. Over the course of my life, I've met many people who love serving and yet were incapable of asking for others' help and service. They only understood half the formula! They obviously receive a tremendous amount of joy, satisfaction, and reward from their acts of service, but they are unwilling or unable to let others receive the same level of joy by serving them.

Serving is a demonstration of profound strength because ultimately you cannot take care of and serve another unless you have the ability to care for yourself. Acts of service can be simple: cleaning your child's room, doing dishes, or picking up a piece of trash on the way to your car. Learning to gain joy from each act of service, regardless of whether it is acknowledged, is the key to living as an evolved pack member. We grow service by daily acts of kindness, compassion, and understanding. To share a laugh and a smile, to help a neighbor with a project, to spend the extra twenty minutes playing with your child—these are the actions we take to grow our service muscle. We demonstrate gratitude for each opportunity to serve, just as we demonstrate gratitude for each time we have been served. Don't lay down your life in service to others out of some sense of guilt; lay down your life in service to others as a profound demonstration of self-love.

My challenge to you is to honor your role as steward of the world you have created. Make sure at day's end your world is brighter and more beautiful because you were here.

IF I CAN STOP ONE HEART FROM BREAKING, I SHALL NOT LIVE IN VAIN; IF I CAN EASE ONE LIFE THE ACHING, OR COOL ONE PAIN, OR HELP ONE FAINTING ROBIN UNTO HIS NEST AGAIN, I SHALL NOT LIVE IN VAIN.

EMILY DICKINSON

Service Exercises

EXERCISE 1.

Simple service: How frequently do you participate in the following acts of service? Next to each item in the list below, write: Usually, Sometimes, Rarely, or Never.

- Picking up a piece of trash _____
- Holding open a door _____
- Volunteering _____
- Giving blood _____
- Helping a neighbor _____
- Mentoring _____
- Donating old clothes and goods _____

EXERCISE 2.

List the service organizations you regularly support with your time.

- _____
- _____
- _____
- _____

EXERCISE 3.

List the service organizations you support financially.

- _____
- _____
- _____
- _____

EXERCISE 4.

If you are employed outside of the home, how many people does your service regularly touch?

* ____1 to 4
* ____5 to 14
* ____15 to 49
* ____50 to 199
* ____200 to 999
* ____1,000 or more

EXERCISE 5.

Could you, would you reach more people with your service? What would it look like?

Success

He has achieved success who has lived well, laughed often,
and loved much;
Who has enjoyed the trust of pure women, the respect of intelligent
men and the love of little children;
Who has filled his niche and accomplished his task;
Who has never lacked appreciation of Earth's beauty or failed to
express it;
Who has left the world better than he found it,
whether an improved poppy, a perfect poem, or a rescued soul;
Who has always looked for the best in others and given them the best
he had;
Whose life was an inspiration;
Whose memory a benediction.

BESSIE ANDERSON STANLEY

T
<u>TRUTH</u>

That which actually is.

WITHOUT TRUTH, THERE CAN BE NO FREEDOM!

WHEN WOULD A reasonable, moral, rational person be willing to die for a lie? Let me tell you a story about a battle from about a century and a half ago.

> On a cold, fog-shrouded morning, frozen corpses lie strewn across the battlefield, trapped forever in their nightmare poses and your memory. Meanwhile, companies, battalions, brigades, and divisions begin to form behind the lines, as each soldier gives up his unique identity to follow his country. You and all your comrades in arms know that today's battle will forever change the face of the nation. Every man on the field prepares to make the ultimate sacrifice. The soldiers find their courage in their belief in the cause; it holds back their fear of failing the men next to them and their fear that the terror in their minds will keep them from doing their duty. As morning light arrives, you hear the muffled sounds of weapons being checked and the whispers of pride, fear, courage, and terror. In the distance, you can see precisely the same actions being taken by your enemies, who are only distinguishable from your comrades by the dark blue color of their uniforms. Horror meets horror, as you notice the colors of your older brother's regiment. You realize that your brother stands on the opposite side of the same field, praying to the same God, asking for the same blessing in the name of righteousness, as he draws his sword to kill you, his brother. Which of you fights for the truth? Does it matter? Will you ever know?

Roll up your sleeves, my friends, because during this dialogue about the truth, we're gonna get dirty!

Truth at Work

For many people in 1492, the world was flat, human beings would never fly, and bleeding the sick was high science. What do we really know about the truth, and why is the truth important? Why are so many of us afraid of the truth, if in fact it will set us free? One of the most powerful and influential organizations in Western culture (where we pride ourselves in our rational, scientific minds) is built upon a bedrock of miracles: a talking serpent, a burning bush, a man who parted the seas in order to lead his people to freedom, a boat that held two of every species on earth within its hull, a virgin who gave birth to God's son, a resurrection that came after a very public execution. What an interesting foundation for a logical, pragmatic culture! Much of the New Testament focuses on the life and teachings of Jesus Christ, and I am convinced that his admonition in John 8:32, "and ye shall know the truth and the truth shall set you free," is one of the most powerful, significant, and under-applied truths of the scriptures.

Why should we bother seeking the truth, when our parents, teachers, spiritual leaders, and politicians will feed it to us? Why must truth be sought? Is it possible that our senses are not to be trusted? Does our ability to rationalize almost any action blind us to the truth?

To help answer these questions, let's look at the two kinds of truth: absolute and relative.

Each of our relative truths emerges from the unique circumstances of our birth and rearing. Try to determine which of the following individuals has access to the truth: a poor black child growing up in Atlanta in the 1960s, a disfigured child growing up in the streets of India during the 1970s, a British prince growing up in the 1980s, or a beautiful girl growing up in Beverly Hills, California, in the 1990s. Imagine the difficulties these people would have communicating or understanding each other. All of us grow up with a unique set of beliefs. These relative truths find daily reinforcement. Whether life is a dream or a living hell will be proven as a truth by the circumstances under which one lives. Our understanding of truth becomes further distorted by social pressure and economic stimuli—the attitudes of those around us and the beliefs fostered by advertising.

If you examine the current state of the world and the quality of people's lives, I think you'll see that a lot of the trouble comes from people basing their actions on truths that bear little relationship to what actually is. Science and technology are changing our relative truth almost daily. The gift of scientific thought is that through it we have learned to challenge everything, assume nothing, and hold no attachments to any outcome. Strange as it seems, this kind of skepticism is the best environment for reaching truth. Imagine the relative truth of living on a flat planet with the sun, moon, and stars all orbiting you; a time when bleeding the sick was considered high science. Contrast that with today's world of quantum physics, space travel, and nanotechnology. In a thousand years, how quaint and backward do you think our current relative truths will appear?

The absolute truth has always been the same—what changes is our ability to access and understand it. We can call it God, universal law, or simply existence, but we will spend much of our lives banging up against, and living discordantly with, absolute truth bruising our bodies, minds, and spirits, until we finally learn humility and gain wisdom. When we live, act, and believe outside of this universal law, we experience pain, anxiety, frustration, and depression. I believe (my relative truth) that these negative emotions stem from our loss of harmony with the ultimate "IS."

OK, that's pretty abstract, but the essential thing to remember is that we should never stop questioning! You never get to stop, but you can find peace in the innate knowledge that, in questioning, searching, and driving for the truth, we will find our joy and freedom. Please don't let "because I say so" be the most frequent answer to your child's questions—his or her brilliant, inquisitive mind deserves better. Help your children become seekers of truth at an early age; teach them the power and freedom that comes with their personal search for truth. If absolute truth really exists, then it is our job to discover what it is with open minds and live in harmony with that understanding.

THE SEARCHING-OUT AND THOROUGH INVESTIGATION OF TRUTH OUGHT TO BE THE PRIMARY STUDY OF MAN.

CICERO

Growing Truth

Beware the man, woman, or institution that claims to be in possession of the truth. Until I can levitate, walk on water, and turn your Evian bottle into a beautiful Santa Ynez Pinot, you had better take everything I write with a healthy grain of salt!

How can we actively grow our experience and understanding of absolute truth? To begin with, doing so requires courage and a willingness to discover how wrong we can be on a regular basis. We must challenge our most deeply held belief systems. A truth seeker will look for flaws, holes, and weaknesses in his current belief system, and most importantly, release any attachment to expected outcomes. Don't allow your identity to become embedded in any single belief system, because as you grow in knowledge, many of your current truths may no longer fit! It's not only impolite, but also counterproductive to become defensive and combative when your belief systems are attacked. Thank God (or whatever you believe in) that you are greater than that which you believe. Relative truth is nothing more than a benchmark of your current level of life experience and understanding. As you grow in experience and wisdom, your relative truths will move closer to the absolute truth. Your ability to rationally, unemotionally, and clearly support and defend your relative truths is a measure of how closely aligned they are to existence.

We have been told never to discuss religion, politics, or sex in polite company. Could it be that these guidelines exist to protect us from many of our own unsupported, underexplored, and unreasoned belief systems? I am amazed at how many people who claim to be religious have little understanding of the basic texts and principles of their own religion. Have you ever met a Republican or Democrat who gleefully spouts his party's talking points without ever fully understanding or challenging them? Religious beliefs or political convictions unsupported by study and reflection aren't worth much. To grow truth, you are obligated to explore the roots of your ideas and beliefs. What happens to truth when any history is translated across cultures, languages, and centuries? How have the teachings been manipulated by politics and power struggles over the centuries? By the way, my point isn't to criticize any particular belief system or replace it with any other—my point is to have you challenge your own beliefs.

Ultimately, growing truth is about reclaiming your spiritual, mental, emotional, and physical harmony. Far too often, we allow some self-proclaimed expert to create our belief systems for us. Be extremely mindful when someone asks you to wear a label signifying a religious or political affiliation. Make sure you have tested and chosen your belief systems, so they are not simply an expression of your upbringing or what others around you want you to think.

Tools In Truth

Just as a pilot checks radio beacons on the VOR system to correct an airplane's course, you can keep checking and correcting your own life's course, so you know where you are headed and you reach your destination safely. Mastery of any skill requires you to stay on course through constant correcting and striving to maintain the straightest course possible toward absolute truth. What are your personal beacons? They're the experts you consult in significant areas of your life. Learn from them, and model your behavior on their behaviors. Then, you will move your belief systems closer to the absolute truth.

Still, you need to be careful about these course corrections, because you can be in harmony with one aspect of your life, while another aspect is tied to a lie. As a trainer and personal coach, I have met men and women who have created beautiful, powerful bodies out of a deep love and respect for this amazing machine. I have also encountered individuals with beautiful, functional, powerful bodies who have developed them to be used as a tool to intimidate and control others. Without genuine harmony between their bodies and spirits, these people are headed for a fall.

Where do these disparities in spirit come from? Sometimes they emerge from the self-confirming beliefs of a misguided group, a phenomenon we call "group-think." The famous story of the emperor with no clothes gives us a fine example of group-think. If enough people say something is so, it becomes a relative truth that masquerades as absolute truth—before you know it, we're all walking around with no clothes on. Growing truth correctly is about testing ideas. Testing a raincoat is easy: if you have worn the coat properly in a storm, but you still got wet, the coat has failed. Practice doing the same thing with different components of your belief system. If people are selling happiness or a spiritual practice, you can begin by observing them. Are they walking their talk? Can you see it working in their lives? If it looks as if they are getting the results you want, then take the belief system out and test it. If it creates what you are looking for, hold onto it; if it doesn't give you the results you want, then let it go.

If peace, joy, and contentment are representative of the aligning with absolute truth, then anxiety, stress, and depression are how the universe tells us we are living outside the truth.

In this chapter's exercises, we're going to try to find out where we have wandered farthest off course in our journey toward truth. We will look at our health—mental, physical, emotional, and spiritual—and our relationship with God, ourselves, family, friends, and community. Finally, we are going to consider our professional levels of satisfaction, service, security, and financial abundance.

No pleasure is comparable to standing upon the vantage-ground of truth.

FRANCIS BACON

Truth Exercises

EXERCISE 1.

Using a high (H), moderate (M), and low (L) scale, review the following, and attach the appropriate rating.

_____ Joy
_____ Peace
_____ Contentment
_____ Anger
_____ Anxiety
_____ Frustration

Health

_____ Mental
_____ Physical
_____ Emotional
_____ Spiritual

Professional

_____ Satisfaction
_____ Service
_____ Security
_____ Financial abundance
_____ Number of people positively affected

EXERCISE 2.

Select a topic you feel passionately about—abortion, religion, politics, unions, war, any subject that gets your pulse pumping—and rate your knowledge of that subject. Is it expert, well informed, general, strong, little?

Now, find a sparring partner. Select an individual you know, trust, and respect, and who has an opposing belief system. Explain to that person that you would like to conduct an intellectual experiment. Your opponent has three minutes to express and justify his or her beliefs in that area. You will listen in absolute silence. Now, trade places and ask your partner to listen for three minutes while you express your views. Then take another five minutes to challenge and question each other's information and beliefs in a respectful debate. Just make sure that both of you maintain a respectful, rational discussion, as free of emotion as possible. If either of you becomes heated, take a minute before resuming your discussion. Review and make notes on your experience of the exercise, paying close attention to how your emotions respond throughout the exercise.

EXERCISE 3.

If you lean right, take a look at Robert Scheer's website, truthdig.com, every day for a week. If you lean left, spend the week with David Frum on frumforum.com. As much as you can, avoid the extreme, overheated versions of your ideological opposite, and see what calm, reasoned arguments from a different perspective look like. The goal is to really listen to the arguments being presented and watch your reactions. Most importantly, have fun with it!

The Guy in the Glass

When you get what you want in your struggle for pelf,
And the world makes you King for a day,
Then go to the mirror and look at yourself,
And see what that guy has to say.

For it isn't your Father, or Mother, or Wife,
Who judgement upon you must pass.
The feller whose verdict counts most in your life
Is the guy staring back from the glass.

He's the feller to please, never mind all the rest,
For he's with you clear up to the end,
And you've passed your most dangerous, difficult test
If the guy in the glass is your friend.

You may be like Jack Horner and "chisel" a plum,
And think you're a wonderful guy,
But the man in the glass says you're only a bum
If you can't look him straight in the eye.

You can fool the whole world down the pathway of years,
And get pats on the back as you pass,
But your final reward will be heartaches and tears
If you've cheated the guy in the glass.

DALE WIMBROW SR.
©1934

U
<u>UNDERSTANDING</u>

Clarity with regard to your own or another's intentions, expectations, and goals.

All Understanding begins and ends with you. Until you are clear on your motivations, intentions, and desires, you can't communicate these to others. Until you care enough to listen deeply to those you care about, you will know no Understanding.

WE CAN NEVER understand other people without first understanding ourselves. Saying I love my wife is an enormous understatement; I adore her. She is as bright as she is beautiful, as loving as she is kind. Her smile and her presence light up a room, making all those around her feel safe, loved, and welcome. I have a dirty little secret—that isn't very secret. There are days when I can't seem to connect on any level. On these days, I don't understand her, and I know she doesn't understand me.

If there are times when I can't understand the woman I love more than life itself, what hope do I have of achieving a successful relationship? Throughout this book, we have thought a great deal about what success looks like in a number of areas, and how to achieve it. By now, I'm sure you have an idea about which single achievement I place above all others in terms of its difficulty, the rewards it bestows, the respect it grants, and the wisdom it imparts. Climbing Mount Everest, running a Fortune 500 company, and earning an Olympic gold medal all pale in comparison to this monumental accomplishment: loving yourself and another person well for the duration of your adult life. That achievement comes from understanding, and it's not easy, but I've seen it done.

I was blessed beyond measure to have been raised by parents who achieved this. Married for sixty-two years, they spent sixty-one of their sixty-two years of marriage together, separated only their last year by a disease that stole my mother's memories, and ultimately, her will to live. My parents lived, loved, argued, and fought. They raised three children together; they suffered the agonizing pain of burying one child together. Most importantly, they achieved a kind of harmony, an understanding of how they fit together as a team. I remember fifty roses on their golden anniversary cake, and sixty roses ten years later, surrounded by handmade cards. Most of all, I remember the sight of them holding hands. I also remember, on occasion, raised voices, slamming doors, and flying objects—usually potted plants aimed at my father's head. They were far from perfect, as was their marriage, and yet I've come to understand perfection isn't really achievable in this area, and shouldn't be the goal. Instead, the goal is to enjoy the ride with someone you love—and, by God, they did that! I have also come to understand how important and difficult all relationships are; they can be the cause of our deepest joys and our most profound hurts. They are also our greatest opportunities for growth.

Understanding at Work

Understanding connects us with our God, our family, our friends, and our world. Understanding comes from a desire to connect with all things. It is a conscious act that requires effort and energy, and a skill that requires daily training and nourishment. When I have an honest understanding of the events and beings around me, I have a positive impact on them. A great farmer who loves and understands the land can create a lifetime of food for himself, his family, and his community. By meeting the needs of the soil he works, this farmer creates a sustainable, mutually beneficial relationship with the land. Mindful farming, including crop rotation and organic amendments, over time, will actually make the soil grow richer and more productive. On the other hand, a farmer who doesn't understand the land can destroy its ability to produce in a few years. When we take the time and expend the effort to know how something or someone works, we are able to create harmonious relationships that benefit everyone. When we have no interest in understanding the people and world around us, we move through life like a plague, destroying instead of creating.

Peak performers seek to understand and meet the needs of their own, body, mind, and spirit, in order to accomplish three important things. First, understanding their needs allows them to achieve their full potential. Second, understanding their own needs enables them to gain insight into the needs of others. Finally, their understanding of their needs enables them to communicate these needs to others. People who have learned to understand and meet their own needs are easy to spot. Their strength, energy, and enthusiasm are magnetic; their peace, joy, and love are clearly visible in shared smiles, helping hands, and the sparkle in their eyes. As peak performers, we learn to operate from a base of health and strength by creating time each week to rest, exercise, play, grieve, and laugh. From this base, you can invest the energy needed to understand others.

To understand another, we must have the strength, desire, and patience to love, listen deeply, and observe. And while gaining an understanding of ourselves, others, and the world around us takes effort, the return is huge. The quality of our lives and the amount of success we experience are directly linked to our understanding of our own wants, needs, and expectations and those of the people around us. Understanding leads to harmony, which in turn leads to creation, expansion, and abundance. Misunderstanding leads to conflict, which leads to destruction, chaos, and misery. Understanding—whether it's of yourself, others, or the land upon which we live—is one of the highest forms of self-expression. When we misunderstand ourselves, others, and our world, we create room for suicide, wars, and pollution.

SPEAK YOUR TRUTH QUIETLY AND CLEARLY; AND LISTEN TO OTHERS, EVEN TO
THE DULL AND IGNORANT, THEY TOO HAVE THEIR STORY.

MAX EHRMAN

Growing Understanding

"No one understands me." "I don't understand me." "I don't understand what she is doing." "What is he thinking?" We worry about understanding. Now it's time to grow our power to understand.

As with every other essential skill, understanding requires clear goals and a consistent plan for their attainment. Before we can understand others, we must discover how to have a healthy, loving relationship with ourselves. If you're unsure of them yourself, then how can you clearly express your wants, needs, desires, and expectations to those around you? Start by removing the obstacles to understanding—but what are those?

First of all, the greatest single impediment to growing understanding is noise! Both literal noise (the sound of our daily lives) and figurative noise (the distractions and daily concerns that occupy us all day) get in the way of the contemplation necessary to grow understanding. It's hard to hear and listen to that wise inner voice when the day is crammed with noise and activity. The alarm goes off; you cook and clean; you grab a cup of coffee, read the paper, and race to the car. Then you turn on the radio, drive to work, review your schedule, read your e-mail, take your meetings, and make your conference calls ... activity never ends. Once you get home, you turn on the TV until it's time to sleep. Tomorrow it happens all over again. Where do you find quiet time? Where is your time for reflection, thought, and understanding? How can you identify what's throwing your life out of balance, when you never make the time to listen and be alone?

Like preparing soil for your garden, budgeting quiet time is the first step on your quest for understanding. Until you are willing to honestly listen to yourself, you have very little chance of hearing others. The next time you have a fight with your spouse, parent, or child: stop! Ask for some time, and then go in search of what's honestly driving your anger. Doing this creates an opportunity for healing and an even higher level of connection with your loved one. For all you know, the fight you had with your wife might have been caused by the jackass who cut you off on the freeway that morning, the bad news you received in the mail, or the sandwich you ate that didn't agree with you. Once we begin fighting, regardless of the cause, real damage is being done to the people we love the most.

Most infant's cries and screams come from a place of frustration, not a place of anger. Why can't daddy understand that I am cold, wet, and hungry? If I only had the words to tell him what I want, I wouldn't be screaming. Aren't most of our arguments coming from the same place of frustration? Why can't my husband understand that I want him to listen and hold me? I don't want sex right now, and I don't want him to fix it! Why can't my wife understand that I want to feel that same sense of connection, passion, and importance we felt before we were married and had kids? I don't expect it every day, but I still really need it. What I find fascinating is that these frustrations and so many others are universal and have been around forever. Yet very few of us ever become proficient enough at communication and understanding to help our spouse get it.

When you have cultivated the power of understanding, you will find balance and harmony much more accessible in your life. Your understanding will aid you in times of suffering too. With the capacity to understand, you will much more easily and effectively achieve your goals because you will have greater clarity. How do you develop this capacity?

The answer is fairly simple: you grow understanding by practicing active listening, the conscious effort to quiet your mind and allow all your senses to receive information. One of the best ways to achieve this state is through meditation. You can use formal meditative exercises, some of which we have explored in earlier chapters, or you can mindfully and consistently create times for quiet contemplation. A thirty-minute nature walk alone (and without portable music) is an excellent place to exercise quiet. Many people are terrified of being alone, and our culture's pace helps support this fear. Once you've adjusted to the silence, you'll find the voice inside yourself reassuring, and you'll develop a habit of finding quiet places.

Once you have developed the ability to listen actively to yourself, begin exercising active listening with others. Think about how other people listen to you for guidance on this part. Some people never listen mindfully; they're wonderful at stepping on others' sentences, listening only to help prove their points, with no desire at all to understand anyone else. Others always seem to understand because they listen well. Active listening takes focus and discipline; your only objective is to understand clearly and connect with another person. Eye contact, silence, and a genuine desire to hear are the only tools you really need as an active listener. Practicing this skill will help the relationships you value the most.

One more thing about understanding—leave the past where it belongs. I wish I had the skill as a writer to show you how timely, challenging, and deeply personal creating some of these performance tips has been. The tragedy is that if you were one of my clients, you would have had no idea because, like a true professional, I don't take my "stuff" into work with me. This created the unfortunate circumstance of having the woman I love most finding herself perfectly positioned behind the sights of my awful mood. I know it's ridiculous to write about the importance of understanding while I'm simultaneously fighting with my wife over some misunderstanding.

During this period of grumpiness, I took frequent time-outs to try to figure out why I was in such a bad mood. I knew I wasn't communicating well with my wife, but it seemed simple to me. All I really wanted was for us to get along, enjoy life, and grow stronger, the way we did a couple of years ago. The most frustrating part of all this madness was that I knew she wanted the same thing. I wanted things to be like they were, if only for a little while—the horseback rides, yoga, concerts, hot dates, and hanging out with my parents! And that's when it hit me; that's when I got it. I had been wishing for the impossible. When my wife and I met, my parents were alive, my daughter's mom was alive, we hadn't been through a horrific legal battle, and we didn't have a baby. Now, we have had three deaths in the family; the legal battle took our savings, but we survived and became a family and; we were hit hard by the recession, like so many other people. Some good things, some bad things, and now we're in a different place. So here I was, wishing for the impossible and blaming my wife because I couldn't have it.

This realization contained the gift of understanding for me. I began working on the present instead of wanting impossible things from the past. To do that, I had to ask an important question: what does our life together look like now? It turned out to be great, and now I'm looking forward to the things that can and will happen, instead of those that already did and can't.

Of all the performance tips we have focused on, understanding is one of the most fun to play with and easiest to develop. Even small improvements in your ability to understand will produce immediate results. Begin exercising your active listening today by creating moments and opportunities for quiet time for yourself and those you are in relationship with, and you will be amazed at how the world opens up for you.

THE IMPROVEMENT OF UNDERSTANDING IS FOR TWO ENDS:
FIRST, OUR OWN INCREASE OF KNOWLEDGE; SECONDLY,
TO ENABLE US TO DELIVER THAT KNOWLEDGE TO OTHERS.

JOHN LOCKE

Understanding Exercises

EXERCISE 1.

Answer these questions:

1. How much daily quiet time do you budget?

_____ 0 to 15 minutes
_____ 15 to 30 minutes
_____ 30 to 45 minutes
_____ More than 45 minutes

2. When you are angry, do you tend to withdraw or become reactive?

3. After an argument, are you quick to recognize your role in the conflict and apologize, or do you tend to focus on how and why you're right and the other person is wrong?

4. Is there a vision of the past that you are holding on to that is preventing you from experiencing your greatest now?

5. In your most significant relationships are you finding yourself having the same arguments over and over again? Take some time to write down what issue keeps coming up, then figure out what the other person is trying to communicate. What have you been unable to hear and understand now that you couldn't before?

_____
_____
_____

EXERCISE 2.

At least once a day, make a commitment to practice active listening, where you are fully engaged in understanding another's experience.

The Old Cat and the Puppy

This morning, like all mornings, the old cat moved to her favorite spot on the couch, where the new day's sunlight brings her warmth inside.

As the old cat curled up with her tail wrapped around her like a furry blanket, the puppy burst into the room and began chasing his tail in endless circles.

The old cat smiled and watched, enjoying the show. The puppy spun himself into exhaustion, rested, panted, and then began spinning again.

After many minutes of this, the old cat stopped licking her paw, looked down at the now tired puppy. She asked him what he was about.

The puppy wagged his tail and announced that he had made a very important discovery. "Old cat" he said, "I have found happiness, and she lives in my tail. If I can only be fast enough and catch her, she will be mine forever."

The old cat purred, smiled, and said, "Puppy, you are very wise, for I too discovered the truth of what you say many years ago. There is just one thing that you have missed."

"What could this be?" puppy asked.

With great wisdom in her eyes, the old cat looked at the puppy and said, "It is true: happiness lives in your tail. If you can just learn to leave her alone, she will gladly follow you wherever you go."

V
<u>VISION</u>

Current and future sight; the power to see possibilities.

Your past doesn't compare to your Vision of the future!

REGARDLESS OF OUR faith (or lack thereof), we were born creative beings, and we are engaged in something creative during each moment we spend on this earth. Our relationships, bodies, self-image, homes, and careers all demonstrate our creative vision at work. Vision is among the most powerful gifts you can have, and one of this book's primary goals is to help you develop it. Every thought, word, and deed drives us to a different reality; making the decisions that bring the reality you want into being requires vision. Everything you have around you, from the clothes you wear to the room you're in, flows in some way from a vision of yourself. We access our greatest potential by learning to harness, direct, and control the power of vision.

Vision can make amazing things possible, as it did for my friend Jason. He has a list of titles that is hard to believe if you haven't met him: pilot, master magician, published author, PhD, deep water diver, expert in martial arts, and a few others he's achieving right now. He is as close to a real James Bond as any man I have ever known. If you met him in 1965, you wouldn't imagine that this shy, awkward, overweight boy would transform himself into a real-world superhero. Jason describes his adolescent years as those of a typical fat kid; he was unmotivated, unpopular, unfit, and a few other "un" things too. This unhappy existence began to change one day when he went to the movies by himself. He saw *Our Man Flint*, a James Bond spoof staring James Coburn as an absurdly suave and multi-talented secret agent. Mesmerized by this cartoon action hero, Jason saw the movie every day for a week and wrote down every amazing skill Flint possessed. His dream was to become like this hero; the dream developed into a much clearer vision of himself with all these skills. Driven by his desire to transform himself, Jason found that he had an indomitable spirit, and he put in the hard work necessary to become the man in his vision.

Jason had discovered an important truth: one of the greatest joys can occur when we touch the divinity lying dormant in each of us and fulfill a beautiful vision of ourselves. Do you still dare to dream? Learn how to convert your most consistent dreams into a vision of yourself and your life. How bold and beautiful is your vision for the next ten years? Let's make it even bigger and brighter.

Vision at Work

In 1970, I was eight years old, and I had a chance to let my imagination run wild. I got to go to a big toy store with a ten dollar bill, which at that time was a fortune. I flew up and down the aisles, lost in a sea of toys, asking myself over and over, "What do I want?" I made my way to the model section, a huge department in toy stores before the electronic age, and I stared in awe at all that I might create. I gazed at rocket ships, race cars, submarines, and battleships, until my eyes locked on a model of a World War II fighter, a Boeing P38 split tail. I loved building airplanes, and I dreamed of learning to fly them one day. Besides, this model was extra special because my dad had worked on the real ones in the Boeing factory. This model was perfect, exactly the one I wanted!

I bought it and built it. Were you waiting for something more momentous than that to happen? Well, here's my point. The store was full of kids asking the same question, "What do I want?" and answering it in different ways. The beauty of this adventure for me was that the vision was my own. None of us share exactly the same vision or exactly the same reasons for having it. Your vision answers the big questions: Who are you? What do you really want? Your goals answer the little questions: What do I need to do get there? What are the steps, the pieces, the components, the information, and the instruction that I need to create my vision? Goals are important—see the goals chapter—but only vision can tell you what you really want.

Vision has been doing wonders in the world for a long time. Our Founding Fathers' vision of a new country, built on the principles of equality and opportunity, gave birth to this nation. Gandhi's vision of an independent India freed his people, and he managed it without having to fight a war with Great Britain. Michelangelo's vision of the human form allowed him to create the statue of David. Vision enables us to tap into universal energy and create a completely new reality for ourselves and others. Vision isn't just daydreaming; when we explore and develop a positive, beautiful vision for our lives and those we love, we accomplish something great. But you should avoid using this power mindlessly and selfishly—negative visions can become nightmarish realities, and history is full of them. Remember, you are here to create a beautiful vision of your life and spend the rest of your days working toward that end. Life is short, so use your divine gift of vision consistently and mindfully to create something that would truly be worthy of a child of God.

Distinguishing vision, that is, the big picture, from specific goals is important in many areas, especially business. In this regard, managers often talk about strategic and tactical efforts. Strategic efforts are about working on the business as a whole and with an eye on the future. Developing new products, creating production systems, and training staff are all strategic efforts. Tactical efforts, on the other hand, are about working in the business as it already exists. Manufacturing, shipping, bookkeeping, and maintenance are essentially tactical efforts—they accomplish the goals already set out in the overall strategy. Experts in strategic work earn from hundreds to thousands of dollars per hour because the wise use of our intellectual capital, or vision, pays the greatest dividends. Tactical workers, those doing the day-to-day work, are compensated at a much lower rate. This model provides us with a great analogy for the difference between vision and goals in our lives. Yes, we've got to get the tactical work done—our jobs, our chores, and everything else that needs doing—but we need to spend some time and effort on strategic work too. What kind of career, education and lifestyle do you really desire? These are vision questions. What college, what major, where will you live and what will you need to achieve these things? These are goal questions. Make sure you don't get so caught up in the pursuit of your goals that you lose sight of your vision. As I've said before, you need daily time for quiet reflection, so that you can develop your visions and ensure that you keep your life moving down the right path.

Remember, you are not trapped in a lousy job, body, or relationship—your lack of vision has placed you in that situation. Forget about difficult circumstances; they are an opportunity, not an excuse. The world is full of men and women who have pulled themselves to unbelievable heights from the most abject situations through the power and clarity of their visions.

Your life begins as a flawless empty canvas; your education, experience, and talent become the paints and brushes you use to create the portrait of your life. Ultimately, your vision colors the picture of who you really are and will ultimately become.

VISION IS THE ART OF SEEING THINGS INVISIBLE.

JONATHAN SWIFT

Growing Vision

In this book, you have been provided with a series of exercises intended to reveal your inherent self-worth and magnificence. Whoever can honestly see herself as a child of God will have a much greater vision for her life than someone who sees herself as worthless. Seeing yourself as worthy creates certain expectations; those expectations lead almost inevitably to certain outcomes. Those with a sense of worthlessness or helplessness will undoubtedly experience less in every aspect of life.

How do you grow your vision muscle? To begin, you must come to appreciate and understand that all of the beauty and glory that surround you, as well as all the information, access, and opportunities present in your world wouldn't exist if you were unworthy. You are blessed with an amazing abundance of opportunity, beauty, and experience because you truly are a child of God. Grow your vision muscle by growing your awareness and gratitude for all of your blessings. Protect your vision by surrounding yourself with others who possess great vision for their lives and great appreciation for their worthiness. Energy is contagious! Surround yourself with negative people, and your vision will shrink; fill your life with positive friends, and your vision will expand.

A simple test of how well you have grown your vision is to answer the following question: Do you believe the best is yet to come, or that the best is behind you? As we discussed in the chapter on truth, whichever answer you choose will turn out to be correct in reality. People with a powerful sense of vision are constantly learning, growing, evolving, and looking forward to life's next great adventure. Those with weak vision muscles tend to feel like life has passed them by.

The steps involved in growing vision are simple, yet profound.

- **Develop confidence and self-worth.** The beauty that many of the world's great religions share is the idea that we are "children of God" and created in the Creators' image. Learn to perceive yourself as a loving, lovable, amazing, worthy, and capable individual.
- **Consistently expose yourself to new ideas and worlds.** By traveling and reading, and by witnessing different lifestyles, professions, and modes of learning, we can find the paths that best suit us.
- **Keep your eyes on the prize.** Whatever your vision might be, whether to become an Olympic athlete, a great humanitarian, or an astronaut, you must surround yourself with information, data, role models, and images of that profession. You must see the vision to create it!
- **Remain flexible.** As you are exposed to new ideas and develop new skills, your vision might change. Maintain enough flexibility to follow your heart, and yet have enough tenacity to stick with your vision through times of difficulty.
- **Apply elbow grease daily.** The best way to get something done is to do it. To make your visions a reality, you need to be working on them constantly.
- **Be extremely mindful and judicious in the use of the phrase "I am."** Every time you use that phrase, you establish a vision of yourself. When you say, "I am fat," "I am strong," "I am beautiful," "I am

ugly," and so on, those ideas become embedded in your mind. Having vision is about becoming what you will be. Saying "I am" tends to freeze things in place or create a self-fulfilling prophecy. How do you help a person become fit and healthy when their vision tells them that they are fat and weak?

+ **Replace negative "I am" statements with positive affirmations.** Affirmations are great tools that can help us rewrite a lifetime of negative programming. "I am fit, focused, and powerful" only sounds strange to the portion of your mind that believes otherwise. Keep saying it until you believe it. Keep believing it and working at it, and it will become true.

EVERY MAN TAKES THE LIMITS OF HIS OWN FIELD OF VISION
FOR THE LIMITS OF THE WORLD.

ARTHUR SCHOPENHAUER

Vision Exercises

EXERCISE 1.
Read a biography on a man or woman you admire who lived a life very different from what you know.

EXERCISE 2.
List three of your consistently used negative "I am" expressions.

1._____
2._____
3._____

EXERCISE 3.
Convert those negatives into opposite positive affirmations. For instance, turn the negative expression, "I am fat," into its opposite, "I am lean and strong."

1._____
2._____
3._____

EXERCISE 4.
List three of your consistently used positive "I am" expressions.

1._____
2._____
3._____

EXERCISE 5.
For this entire week pay attention to all of your "I am" expressions and those of the people you know. Find out if you have created a primarily positive or negative self-image.

The Higher Pantheism

The sun, the moon, the stars, the seas, the hills and the plains,
Are not these, O Soul, the Vision of Him who reigns?
Is not the Vision He, tho' He be not that which He seems?
Dreams are true while they last, and do we not live in dreams?
Earth, these solid stars, this weight of body and limb,
Are they not sign and symbol of thy division from Him?
Dark is the world to thee; thyself art the reason why,
For is He not all but thou, that hast power to feel "I am I"?
Glory about thee, without thee; and thou fulfillest thy doom,
Making Him broken gleams and a stifled splendour and gloom.
Speak to Him, thou, for He hears, and Spirit with Spirit can meet—
Closer is He than breathing, and nearer than hands and feet.
God is law, say the wise; O soul, and let us rejoice,
For if He thunder by law the thunder is yet His voice.
Law is God, say some; no God at all, says the fool,
For all we have power to see is a straight staff bent in a pool;
And the ear of man cannot hear, and the eye of man cannot see;
But if we could see and hear, this Vision—were it not He?

ALFRED, LORD TENNYSON

WISDOM

Action driven by a healthy heart and keen intellect.

IF I COULD BESTOW ONE GIFT ON YOU IT WOULD BE THE WISDOM TO SPEND YOUR LIFE IN THE PURSUIT OF PEOPLE, ACTIVITIES, AND CAREERS THAT FILL YOUR BODY, MIND, AND SPIRIT WITH JOY.

WISDOM, LIKE BEAUTY, is difficult to describe but easy to recognize when you are in its presence. To be honest, any attempt to encapsulate and teach wisdom as one chapter in this book requires more brain power than I currently possess. Although I have occasionally experienced moments of clarity and insight that approached wisdom, I have also had times when people I admire and respect have looked at me and thought, "What an idiot!" and they have been absolutely right.

From over twenty years of research, study, and observation, I have concluded wisdom is not a skill we can possess consistently, but a relatively rare moment of clarity, connection, and understanding we can strive to touch. Like health and fitness, wisdom requires training and nurturing. Just as we will never achieve absolutely perfect health, we will never attain total wisdom. A large part of our capacity for wisdom comes from our love of the process of becoming wiser, and that fact alone attests to how difficult achieving wisdom truly is. Exercise really isn't about our results or our appearance; the real benefits of exercise emerge in the process of forging, maintaining, and playing with a strong, healthy, beautiful body. A life master pursues wisdom from the same perspective. Our personal wisdom isn't about being recognized for the profundity of our judgments; it's about daily self-expression, self-definition, and self-exploration, guided by the light of an engaged heart and a well-developed intellect.

Wisdom at Work

Combining heart and head to find wisdom isn't easy—especially around here. The tendency toward specialization inherent in Western culture tends to isolate different aspects of our humanity. Our intellects, emotions, bodies, and spirits end up in distinct and separate disciplines. Universities award degrees that focus on these different areas of our being, as if any one of them could function without the other. Wisdom is a very personal expression of our individual humanity acting synergistically with all that we are and all that surrounds us. How do we bring these capacities together?

Because wisdom is such a deeply personal experience, I've decided to use a different teaching approach in this chapter. Instead of providing examples of wisdom at work and sharing tips on how best to grow wisdom, I will provide you with a palette of wisdom seed thoughts. Each is an idea that when nurtured, employed, and adopted will help you experience wisdom from a very personal place. Please feel free to add to the list with seed thoughts of your own.

SCIENCE IS ORGANIZED KNOWLEDGE. WISDOM IS ORGANIZED LIFE.

IMMANUEL KANT

Growing Wisdom

I CRIED BECAUSE I HAD NO SHOES, UNTIL I SAW A BOY WHO HAD NO FEET.

I could retire if I had been given a dollar every time I heard my mom say this, and yet over the years this seed thought has become one of my most effective attitude adjusters. I don't know anyone over the age of eleven who isn't, has not been, or isn't about to be dealing with some major issue, whether real or imagined. As bad as we think things are, someone out there is suffering through even greater challenges, and many times with more grace and dignity than we are demonstrating about our ability to keep things in perspective.

IF YOU THINK YOU CAN'T, YOU MUST!

The things we can and cannot do in this lifetime are rarely predetermined. Train yourself to combat fear with commitment. Learn to drive through your doubts. As Richard Bach so eloquently stated in *Illusions*, "Argue for your limitations, and sure enough, they're yours." Practice silencing that little voice in your head telling you that you can't, or that you're not good enough. When given the chance, always take your swing at bat!

A LASER BEAM WILL GET YOU THERE FASTER THAN A LIGHT BULB.

When you have set yourself to a task, learn to direct all of your physical, mental, emotional, and spiritual energies to that end. Great achievement is driven by consistently directed energy. If things aren't flowing, take a break, and then dive back in when you can be fully present.

FEAR OF FAILURE DOESN'T EXIST.

If fear of failing keeps you from taking action, you have already failed! This acknowledgement should then free you to risk action to reach for your goal. After all, you have nothing to lose (you already lost it) and you might have a 10 percent, 25 percent, or 50 percent chance of success. Who knows? She might say yes; you could be exactly who they are looking for; and somebody has to win!

YOU ARE A MIRACLE, ACT LIKE ONE.

Take some time and reflect on how hard the universe had to work to bring you into being. An infinite number of events had to line up to prepare for, and create, your arrival (I think this is why I love birthdays so much). Now take a look at all the teachers, resources, friends, and opportunities that are waiting and available for you every day. Make it a priority to budget time for your growth and development. Be willing to invest as much time in caring for yourself as you spend taking care of your things. You are a miracle, and it really is time you started acting like one. Always remember, you are worthy!

LEARN TO PLAY AT LIFE; WORK IS TOO TIRING.

I had a great martial arts instructor who began each training session with the command, "Let's play." Strangely enough, he used this instruction when we were learning how to deal with life and death scenarios. The lesson he wanted us to learn was that while the training was deadly serious, we shouldn't take ourselves too seriously. Love, learn, and laugh at your mistakes and at yourself. Life is much easier when you play at it.

BIRTH AND DEATH ARE THE GREAT EQUALIZERS.

We all come into this world and leave it in exactly this same way. I have had the privilege of witnessing three human births, and each one was painful, messy, profound, and the most joyous event I have ever experienced. I have buried a sister, my daughter's mother, and both of my parents, and each death was painful, messy, profound and the most heart-wrenching event I have ever experienced. At the beginning and end of life, "no-thing" matters except our deep desire for love. Everything else we do is just about stuff. Trust me—the only value stuff has for any of us is its ability to help relationships. Be careful—stuff usually gets in the way of our ability to touch and be touched by others.

LIFE IS NOT A SPECTATOR SPORT.

Life is always much more rewarding for participants than for spectators. Many years ago, I found myself in a bar in Ohio during the playoffs with a very wise friend. Someone on TV scored a touchdown, and the entire bar erupted. At that moment, my friend said, "That was one of the saddest things I have ever seen." I asked him what he meant—everybody seemed to be having a good time. He replied, "They're all high fiving each other and saying 'we just scored.' No one here has done anything but drink beer!" He was right. Not one person in front of that TV knew what it felt like to score a touchdown as a pro in front of tens of thousands of screaming fans. Not one person in that bar was playing a game they loved at the highest level possible. I don't mind catching a game on TV once in a while, but in sports and in life, it's much better to play than to watch!

SET RULES THAT YOU CAN WIN BY, BUT STILL MAKE THEM CHALLENGING ENOUGH THAT YOU LOSE ABOUT 35 PERCENT OF THE TIME.

Life really is a game, and although many of its rules are universal (gravity and taxes come to mind), in most cases, whether you are winning or losing at life is a matter of perception—you make the rules and keep the score. You get to define success and find joy in your achievements. At the end of the game, only you will know how well you played it and whether you won. Create the habit of winning around 65 percent of the time. Doing so helps you develop the expectation of winning. If you lose around 35 percent of the time, you'll push yourself hard enough to cause real growth—win too often, and it gets too easy.

HONOR EACH OF LIFE'S EXPERIENCES AND EMOTIONS.

A life well lived will know agonies and ecstasies. We may hear about happiness as the end-all, have-all, but in reality, chasing short-term happiness over long-term Joy—what we think will bring happiness—is as empty as a one-note song. Life's beauty comes from the full range of experiences and emotions that we can have. When we live honestly, we learn to direct and control those emotions when necessary, but more importantly, we learn to feel, own, and express honest emotions.

YOU'RE NOT OLD UNTIL YOU SAY SO.

I have met twenty year olds who have had the capacity to dream, laugh, and play beaten out of them—if it ever existed—and I have met ninety year olds whose energy, enthusiasm, and passion could light up a small town. Old is not a location in time and space; old is an attitude, a surrendering of your inner child. Hold on to the part of you that can still see magic in a rainbow, find fairies at sunset, and honestly believe that your best day is tomorrow! You choose; you decide; you say when you're old!

TRADITION AND RITUAL WITHOUT INTENTION, UNDER-STANDING, AND EXPERIENCE ARE DEAD THINGS.

Great tradition and great ritual flow from great experience. They are man's attempt to preserve, teach, and transfer profound and beautiful experiences.

When the experience is kept alive through the tradition, then you should honor it. When the tradition and ritual take on significance for their own sake, the experience is lost and the traditions and rituals should be destroyed!

OUR CHILDREN DON'T WANT AND NEED THINGS; THEY WANT AND NEED US.

One of the most heartbreaking aspects of coaching executive groups around the country was witnessing the cultural paradigm so many business leaders have been enrolled in. These men and women are working sixty- to ninety-hour weeks; most are out of shape, on blood pressure meds, and literally killing themselves trying to add a point to the company's bottom line. But you discover the heartbreak when you ask them why they do it. The almost universal answer is, "I'm doing it for my family." That's an odd thing to say, because very few families survive climbing the corporate ladder intact. How many first steps, words, and bike rides are you forced to miss when you are never home? After pouring all of your energy into a career, how much juice will you have left to pour into your family? Our children don't care about cars, square footage, or designer anything; they have their priorities straight. They care about us!

NEVER STOP CELEBRATING.

I have an old Marine friend whom I asked one day how he was doing, and his response was, "Any day I'm looking down on the grass instead of the other way around is a great day." Look for reasons to celebrate life. Celebrate the fact that you're still here and that the sky is still blue. Have some fun!

The finish line is in sight. The fact that you have persevered and forged on through each chapter and exercise brings me more joy than you can imagine!

WISDOM IS THE SUPREME PART OF HAPPINESS.

SOPHOCLES

Wisdom Exercises

EXERCISE 1.
Select the one seed thought that will create the greatest benefit for you. Plant it now by writing it down.

EXERCISE 2.
Make four copies of the seed thought. Put one on your nightstand, another on your refrigerator, a third on your desk, and the last one in your organizer.

EXERCISE 3.
For the next seven days, make reading, discussing, and acting on this seed thought a priority. Talk about it with your spouse, friends, and children. Find examples of when acting wisely and applying this seed thought has created joy in your life. Look for situations where not applying this seed thought has cost you or someone you know personally.

EXERCISE 4.
Give back. E-mail me one of your favorite personal seed thoughts, along with a brief explanation of its meaning and how you use it. Let's see if you make it into my next book!

The Tables Turned

Up! up! my Friend, and quit your books;
Or surely you'll grow double:
Up! up! my Friend, and clear your looks;
Why all this toil and trouble?

The sun above the mountain's head,
A freshening lustre mellow
Through all the long green fields has spread,
His first sweet evening yellow.

Books! 'tis a dull and endless strife:
Come, hear the woodland linnet,
How sweet his music! on my life,
There's more of wisdom in it.

And hark! how blithe the throstle sings!
He, too, is no mean preacher:
Come forth into the light of things,
Let Nature be your Teacher.

She has a world of ready wealth,
Our minds and hearts to bless—
Spontaneous wisdom breathed by health,
Truth breathed by cheerfulness.

One impulse from a vernal wood
May teach you more of man,
Of moral evil and of good,
Than all the sages can.

Sweet is the lore which Nature brings;
Our meddling intellect
Mis-shapes the beauteous forms of things:—
We murder to dissect.

Enough of Science and of Art;
Close up those barren leaves;
Come forth, and bring with you a heart
That watches and receives.

WILLIAM WORDSWORTH

X
<u>X-TRA MILE</u>

Consistently expecting more and giving more than is required.

FAT, DUMB, MEAN, AND POOR ARE EASY. STRONG , SMART, LOVING AND
WEALTHY ARE ALL CHILDREN OF HARD WORK. IN ORDER TO LIVE AN
EXTRAORDINARY LIFE, BE PREPARED TO GO THE X-TRA MILE EVERY DAY!

NATURE HAS A way of culling her herds, ensuring survival of the fittest by allowing the weak and infirm to fall away from the pack and become food for her predators. Success does the same thing, but take heart—the fact that you have made it this far tilts the odds of great achievement well in your favor. The world's garages are packed tight with unused exercise equipment, gathering dust and serving as storage racks for more of yesterday's junk. Often, wonderful books on empowerment end up as glorified paperweights or lie unread on a table at some garage sale. For exactly that reason, I saved one of the true secrets of great achievement for the end of this book—I wanted to reward the readers who go the extra mile and finish what they start. To put it bluntly, I wanted to save this ingredient for success for exactly those people who would appreciate and apply it.

In order to achieve great and lasting success in any important endeavor—relationships, health, finances, or career—you must be willing to expect more and give more of yourself than anyone else. You must be willing to go the extra mile!

That's it; that's really all you need to know. There is no magic pill or fairy godmother that is going to come along and make your dreams come true. So, "Cowboy Up," stop complaining, roll up your sleeves, and go to work! Since 1988, I have served as a performance coach in venues ranging from the corporate boardroom, to the shooting range, to the gym, to the backcountry. I have coached multi-millionaires, Navy Seals, actors, stay-at-home mothers, and athletes. Without exception, they achieved great results only through great effort. I've seen talent fail. I've seen looks and brains fail. I've seen money and power fail. Rarely, and I mean rarely, have I seen dogged determination, coupled with a willingness to go the extra-mile, fail.

The X-tra Mile at Work

We all want to succeed, and we want the people we love to do the same. How do we act on the knowledge we possess? How do we help inspire others to reach their potential? I am convinced that one of the greatest challenges we face is the natural lag time that tends to exist between choice and consequence. I vividly remember my mom's all-too-frequent and screechy lectures about the dangers of poor grades. They began in earnest my freshman year of high school and followed me throughout my college career. I wasn't stupid; I couldn't see the value behind mastering what I believed were so many inane exercises. Today, I have a very different perspective. I've come to understand that the reason mom's lectures (God rest her soul) had no effect is that those dangers were nowhere in sight, although they were very real, and boy, did they hurt when they caught up with me. I didn't change my behavior because I had no connection to the pain my actions, or lack of them, would ultimately cause me!

The same is true of dieting. We blather on and on about our increasing obesity rates, yet most people are completely disconnected from the newly expanded butt and stomach they create with every meal. If the calories went directly from our mouths to our backsides, our eating and exercise habits would change instantly!

The opposite is true too—when action and consequence are closely linked, we learn quickly. That is what I call "the truth of the blade." Knife-fighting students begin their training with wooden knives and eventually work up to dulled-edge steel. The attacks begin as quarter-speed pre-choreographed strikes and progress to full speed attacks coming from any position or angle. In close-quarter combat, unlike so much of life, the lag time between choice and consequence is almost instantaneous. Even in the training hall, a bad choice could cost you an eye, broken ribs, or a concussion. It only takes one or two errors in judgment, instantly followed by pain, to focus your energies and create a highly motivated student.

If the consequence of losing is death, you quickly develop a willingness to go the extra mile to win. You gladly move through your katas (fight sequences) hundreds and hundreds of times in slow motion, correcting constantly. You perfect your distance, timing, balance, hand placement, and counterattacks. As new skills develop, you begin slowly accelerating the speed, frequency, and direction of attacks. Your body and nervous system begin moving more efficiently; your mind sharpens too, as you are forced to stay engaged despite fatigue. When you are not actually training, you run through the sequences in your mind, visualizing, repeating, winning, and repeating. Knife fighters invest thousands of hours in this process, because in a knife fight, failure is not an option! There is no room for sloppy, unfocused, undisciplined practice. If you are not fully committed, go home, because at this level of training you are as much a danger to your partners as you are to yourself. At this point, you don't *go* the extra-mile; you *are* the extra-mile! You have made the decision to do anything and everything necessary to master your craft. One day, after countless hours of training, you wake up a very different person. You walk, speak, and move with a new level of grace and confidence. Warrior is no longer a term you read in a book—a warrior is what you are. You are ready for your exam, and you are ready for the real thing. Once you know this feeling deep in your soul, you already know the outcome—you will win!

This is the extra mile at work!

AND WHOEVER COMPELS YOU TO GO ONE MILE, GO WITH HIM TWO.

JESUS OF NAZARETH

Growing the X-tra Mile

In each chapter, we focused on techniques to help us develop an essential strength or skill set. Whatever strength we choose to develop, whether it is our biceps muscle, our courage, or our personal power, it will become stronger only in response to negative resistance, that is, pain, work, and adversity. Everything we value in our character becomes stronger through adaptation to negative resistance, a phenomenon known as the "specific adaptation principle" (SAP). This phrase simply means that it takes negative stimulation (work, labor, effort), not positive (couch, movie, beer), to cause growth. The amount of growth we experience will be determined by our circumstances and our unique ability to manage and effectively adapt to negative stimulation.

Whatever loads or pressures we consistently place on our bodies will over time force them to adapt to meet those demands. This is how, over the course of ten thousand hours, we can take a wobbly, shaky, toddler and through progressively greater challenges (negative stimulation) end up with a world class gymnast, capable of back flips, front flips, and hand stands on a four-inch wide beam suspended three feet above the ground.

The key to effectively applying this principle is managing the size of the load. Too light a load will not stress us enough to stimulate growth; too great a load will stress us to the point of injury. In weight training, we are generally looking for loads that will cause specific muscle groups to fail within a range of four to twenty repetitions. Then you rest and feed the stressed muscle groups because muscular growth doesn't take place during exercise, but in the twenty-four to forty-eight hours of rest afterward. When you repeat this cycle consistently over time, you get larger, stronger muscles. Intellectual development follows a similar pattern; we exchange weights and cardio equipment for books and problem solving. I am convinced that emotional and spiritual growth involves a similar process. The challenge in all these areas is in developing a training regime that will allow for consistent growth. Fortunately, the universe will always find plenty of ways to challenge you emotionally and spiritually. The universal component that determines the outcome of all these processes is work. Your work. It's your life, your mind, your body, and your adventure; no one can go the extra mile for you. You have to walk it alone!

Yes, alone—even while you spend time in the company of wonderful people. Crowds love mediocrity; greatness is for the few, and only you know how great you can be. Ultimately, you aren't performing to please your boss, your partner, teammates, or spouse. You are performing for the man or woman in the mirror! You drive and shine because it is who and what you are. We grow the extra-mile by removing the time stealers in our lives and investing our time and energies in the things that matter most. We pursue our passion, and in doing what we love, we find the strength and desire to do more and more. We grow the extra-mile by seeing and connecting to the thread that exists between our choices and their consequences. We learn to feel the pain of a lesser choice now instead of years into our future, and we let that pain drive us to a better choice. We become psychic knife fighters who play, study, and train as if our lives really did depend on it.

What are you waiting for? Do it now, whatever it is, because the end really is coming. With all my heart, I want all of our ends, middles, and beginnings to be amazing! Here's a list of tips on going that extra mile—get them under way immediately!

+ Always, always, always, show up and show up early. Being on time means you are there ten minutes ahead of the clock, giving yourself time to mentally and physically prepare for the task at hand.
+ Take pride and ownership in all that you do, whether you are the janitor or the CEO of the company, constantly ask yourself how you can make it better.
+ You have much more power than you think you do—use it.
+ Cultivate steady improvement. You are only as valuable to the team as you are powerful, so constantly seek out further education and condition your body, mind, and spirit.
+ Get it done! Push, pull, go over it, go around it, blow it up—no excuses; no one cares, just get it done!

No one ever attains very eminent success by simply doing what is required of him; it is the amount and excellence of what is over and above the required that determines the greatness of ultimate distinction.

CHARLES FRANCIS ADAMS

X-tra Mile Exercises

EXERCISE 1.
Who comes to mind in your life as the embodiment of going the extra mile?

EXERCISE 2.
How does their behavior differ from other people you interact with?

EXERCISE 3.
How has going the extra mile consistently benefited this person?

EXERCISE 4.
What costs do they have to pay in order to go the extra mile?

EXERCISE 5.
This week, make a commitment to be ten minutes early for every meeting and appointment you have on your calendar. Bring your ABC manual, so if you're early and prepared you can be working on your personal development exercises and journal.

EXERCISE 6.
Rent and watch the movie *Rudy* with your family. It will show you what it means to go the extra mile. It was mandatory viewing for all of my black belt candidates before their final exam.

Man in the Arena

It is not the critic who counts; not the man who points out how the strong man stumbles, or where the doer of deeds could have done them better. The credit belongs to the man who is actually in the arena, whose face is marred by dust and sweat and blood; who strives valiantly; who errs, who comes short again and again, because there is no effort without error and shortcoming; but who does actually strive to do the deeds; who knows great enthusiasms, the great devotions; who spends himself in a worthy cause; who at the best knows in the end the triumph of high achievement, and who at the worst, if he fails, at least fails while daring greatly, so that his place shall never be with those cold and timid souls who neither know victory nor defeat.

THEODORE ROOSEVELT

Y
<u>YES</u>

*Embracing, accepting, and affirming all the great things
and people that life has to offer.*

If God and the universe had intended for you to live a small unre-
markable life, then they wouldn't have blessed you with such an
amazing body, mind, and spirit. Learn to say YES to the brilliance
that is your destiny!

BY THIS POINT in our journey, we have learned to say no to a lot of things. We have said no to time stealers, over-packed schedules, negative people, and negative attitudes. You have worked your way through the previous twenty-four chapters and developed a huge tool box of improved strengths and skill sets. Now it's time for a resounding YES! Yes to life, dreams, passion, to enjoying this ride as much as we possibly can. We say yes to accepting our birthright as children of God and creating a life of beauty, joy, and abundance. It's time for an energetic shift from, "I just can't" to, "Yes, I can"!

Let me tell you about my best yes ever. I went on a double blind date—it was the first one I had ever heard of, and definitely the first one I had ever been on. The whole thing felt a little strange, but once I met Robin, it was amazing—I can't think of another time it felt so good just to be with someone. We ended up calling each other on the recommendation of a client's friend. We arranged for our first meeting to be in front of a cowboy bar in the small town near my ranch, and that we'd recognize each other by the color of our shirts: mine, black; hers, green. As I drove there, I realized that neither of us had asked anything about looks—just shirt color. There I stood in the midst of a sea of black shirts, when it happened: I saw a woman in green looking everywhere while talking to me on her cell. She was absolutely breathtaking; I quietly walked up behind her, tapped her shoulder ... and she smiled. Once I was able to catch my breath, I heard a voice that I hadn't heard in a very long time ... it was my soul, saying, "YES! YES! YES!"

Yes at Work

Every philosophy has some sort of duality: good and evil, Yin and Yang, hard and soft, Yes and No. In this discussion, "Yes" represents our capacity for expansion, creation, and growth; "No" represents shrinking, waste, closing off, and diminishing energy. These dualities are easy to see as forces in conflict, but we should remember that they can also complement each other. Yes can drive great achievement: the incandescent light bulb, space travel, the discovery of the New World, and great advances in technology and medicine, for instance. But no has served as an equal partner in many cases. To achieve great things, we must learn to use the power of yes, while simultaneously employing the active and judicious use of no. Say yes to new opportunities. Say yes to things that empower us.

Say yes to our dreams. And say no to time stealers. Say no to self-doubt. Say no to wasted energy. Say no to fear of the unknown.

Yes functions as the driver of confidence, high achievement, and ambitious goals. "Yes, I can! Yes, I will! Yes, I am!" Learning to use yes as a life-enhancing tool should begin at birth. The ratio of yes to no we experience growing up affects our willingness to take risks and ultimately determines the scale of our visions and strengths. Grow a child in an environment dominated by no and you will succeed in shrinking that child's drive, confidence, and spirit. When you say yes to one thing, you must say no to another. By saying yes to freedom and adventure, you are saying no to the known and comfortable. When an entrepreneur says yes to opportunity, she says no to security. When we say yes to a healthy lifestyle, we are saying no to poor eating habits and endless sitting on the couch. Yes allows us to be big, bold, and exciting, to stretch, create, and reach for the stars. Yes will not guarantee success; in fact, yes exposes us to greater risk taking and more failure. Swinging at the ball will never guarantee you a home run. But by not taking your chance at bat, by not saying yes to your turn at the plate, you are guaranteed to fail.

SOME MEN SEE THINGS AS THEY ARE AND SAY, WHY? I DREAM THINGS THAT NEVER WERE AND SAY, WHY NOT?

GEORGE BERNARD SHAW

Growing Yes

Every yes must be grown in a bed of nos. It's time to take out your calendar and attack it with pruning shears. Cut, cut, cut right now; remove unnecessary activities and people from your life. That's right—in addition to cutting unimportant activities from your schedule, you should cut people from your life. It's too short to spend with people who are small minded and negative. Guard your human interactions as jealously as your time; do everything in your power to spend your time with those that add to life's beauty and joy. Review your most important roles—parent, child, community member, human being—and remove anyone and anything that doesn't contribute to your vision for your life. Start growing yes today by perfecting the art of saying no. Begin immediately freeing up your time and energy in order to make space for your next big YES!

Desiring the best for ourselves and loved ones, why and when would we choose a lesser path? Life is a never ending series of Yes and No choices and we define ourselves daily with each one. On your quest for more joy, personal power, and greater life experiences, you grow the big yeses by learning to say no.

The fact that I or anyone else believes in you is irrelevant, until you learn to embrace your magnificence, saying yes to the life you deserve will always be a challenge.

TWENTY YEARS FROM NOW, YOU WILL BE MORE DISAPPOINTED BY THE THINGS THAT YOU DIDN'T DO THAN BY THE ONES YOU DID DO. SO THROW OFF THE BOWLINES. SAIL AWAY FROM THE SAFE HARBOR. CATCH THE TRADE WINDS IN YOUR SAILS. EXPLORE. DREAM. DISCOVER.

MARK TWAIN

Yes Exercises

EXERCISE 1.

Move away from the back of your chair, lengthen your spine, relax your shoulders, bring your chin down slightly, and close your eyes. After taking nine centering breaths, in through your nose and out from your mouth, answer the following questions: What was one of the biggest yes moments of your life? How old were you? What were some of the risks involved? What got you there? What did you gain?

_____

_____

_____

_____

EXERCISE 2.

Do you have, on average, between one and two hours a day scheduled for quiet time, re-creation, reflection, play, and exercise?

EXERCISE 3.

What activities or people do you currently have in your life that do not feed and improve its quality? What can you remove from your calendar?

_____

_____

EXERCISE 4.

How good are you at saying no to time stealers, unnecessary events, people, and over extending yourself?

_____ I'm terrible; I am constantly over extended and overwhelmed.

_____ Not bad; I can say no when I begin to feel overwhelmed.

_____ Pretty good; I can say no to things that really take me away from what's important.

_____ Great; I value and guard my time like Fort Knox.

Exercise 5.

Return to your meditative posture, and after nine focused breaths, answer the following question: What is my next big yes?

_____

_____

_____

Exercise 6.

How will I have to use my power of no to create this?

_____

_____

_____

Exercise 7.

What are two actions I can take right now to start moving this yes forward?

_____

_____

_____

Exercise 8.

In your daily moments of choice, train yourself to ask the following question: What would the most magnificent version of myself do now? You will find that knowing your highest choice suddenly becomes much easier than you have imagined!

Live in Joy

Live in Joy, In love,
Even among those who hate.

Live in Joy, In health,
Even among the afflicted.

Live in Joy, In peace,
Even among the troubled.

Look within. Be still.
Free from fear and attachment,
Know the sweet joy of living in the way.

BUDDHA

Z
<u>ZENITH</u>

High point, culminating point, the end, and the beginning.

MAYBE YOU'RE WAITING FOR YOUR HIGHEST POINT IN LIFE TO ARRIVE
ONE DAY SOON, BUT IMAGINE YOUR LIFE IF YOU STRIVE TO MAKE EVERYDAY
YOUR ZENITH!

I'VE NEVER KNOWN an ending that hasn't been attached to some great new beginning. As we wrap up our journey together, I find myself extremely conflicted. I am full of joy and gratitude for your company on this path of self-discovery and creation; I am relieved to know that we have made it to this summit; I am already nostalgic for the process that got us here, and I can't wait to start our next big adventure. Right around the "L" chapter, an idea crept into my cranium that I couldn't shake; I saw myself finishing our quest at the Santa Barbara Cemetery. There are a lot of reasons this space is important to me (it is my parents' final resting place, for instance), but I think I really wanted to see how much light we could draw from a place people tend to think of as dark!

Here I find myself at the end of a process I have poured as much love and effort into as anything in this life. I've arrived at the cemetery, and it's funny in that weird Hollywood way, but the day I have scheduled to write "Z" is right out of a Hitchcock film. I know it sounds like a cliché, but it is a cold, damp, foggy, June morning. My workspace is a century old, beautiful bench carved from granite that doubles as a lookout point and a family tombstone. The Channel Islands are somewhere off in the fog, the ships anchored in the harbor rock listlessly like small, mismatched metronomes. Although I'm wearing a jacket, I feel the cool morning breeze and damp deep in my bones. A cemetery might seem an odd place to write the final chapter of a book written with the intention of making our lives as big, bright, and beautiful as possible. After losing so many loved ones over the years, I have found that death has actually become one of my muses. We need the night to appreciate each new day, and we need death to make us embrace and honor the fleeting moments of life we receive.

As you know by now, my dad, a former aerospace engineer, passed away from cancer. A few months before he died, we were able to arrange a flight in a World War II T-28 aircraft carrier trainer. The pilot flew my dad over my dad's ranch, his old boarding school, and many of his favorite childhood haunts. They did a couple of barrel rolls and even a flyby (at a tower-free airport). After the flight, we all went to lunch. Throughout lunch, all my dad kept saying was, "This is my best day. I can't believe it. Wow! This is my best day." This came from a man with a body riddled with cancer. Understand this and you have gained one of the most important keys of this entire book!

Zenith at Work

Why do we need death? It's because knowing where my story ultimately ends drives me to make the middle and final chapters as beautiful as I possibly can. I am a man of great faith; I find it inconceivable that the beauty and order that make up this universe are the result of some great cosmic accident, yet I am also a realist, and I understand that the end my life really is the end. It is with this knowledge that I have struggled to teach, motivate, coach, cajole, and drive all of us to a zenith that is bigger and brighter. Because life is now, it is our ultimate creation, gift, and responsibility.

My inescapable mortality gives me a sense of urgency that drives me to make positive change a reality in my life and help you do the same in yours. Our mortality reminds us to be present. We can't afford to pass up the chance to hold those that we love, to help a neighbor or friend, or to make someone's burden a little bit lighter. I personally will not go quietly into this dark night, I will rage against the age, and I will demonstrate my rage through a celebration of life, of joy, of passion, of loving. I know my struggle is really nothing more than a delaying tactic, but delay I will. I will use exercise, nutrition, and my attitude to keep the reaper at bay for as long as I can. I will fight gravity; I will fight old age; I will fight inertia. I will hold on to youth, energy, passion, playfulness and magic. When the fight is over, I hope to leave this adventure with grace and dignity, and I also intend to be completely spent. It is my fondest wish that each day be my zenith, to be present and born anew with each dawn.

Honestly, what are you waiting for? When will you pick up your mantle of brilliance? When will you walk, talk, act, and live as a child of God? What are you waiting for? Yesterday is history; tomorrow is a mystery—that's why today is our present and should be enjoyed like one!

Thank you for sharing this adventure with me, for driving me to find the words, and most of all, for sticking with it and growing with me through this wonderful process. I pray that this book follows my vision for my life and ends its days tattered and torn, loved and worn, dog-eared, highlighted, scribbled on, and shared. Use this book up, use the exercises, use the information, and let them be focal points and tools for developing your power and your genius. Go back and review your notes and exercises over the years. As you grow and change, watch how the exercises grow and change with you.

I was deeply honored when asked to be keynote speaker at my eldest daughter, Miranda's, graduation. For the past ten years or so, I have had this recurring fantasy: I travel back in time to my high school graduation and give the seventeen-year-old me some of the hard-earned wisdom and insights I've gleaned over the past thirty years. Since I haven't figured out how to do this yet, I thought I might try sharing those insights with the graduating class of 2010. I think the five seed thoughts I came up with will serve as an ideal close for this book. These chapters have been designed to help you build your life skills tool box and in doing so prepare you for every adventure, challenge, and opportunity that comes your way. These final thoughts are meant to assist you in maintaining your perspective and directing your energies to your life's many zeniths.

IT IS A MISTAKE TO LOOK TOO FAR AHEAD. ONLY ONE LINK OF THE CHAIN OF DESTINY CAN BE HANDLED AT A TIME.

WINSTON CHURCHILL

Growing to Your Zenith

LIFE IS HARD—HARD IS NOT BAD!

It doesn't take us to long to realize that life is hard and the reality is nothing like the Disney movies we were raised on. Bullies, acne, mean teachers, and clueless parents are everywhere. There's a fierce pecking order in the school, and none of us really understanding any of the rules of life. Somewhere along the line we get this bright idea that if we could get out of wherever we are, everything would be great. We rush to get out of high school and into college. Well, it turns out college can be really hard, and the kids aren't very different than the ones we knew in high school, so we can't wait to get out of college and start working. Our first job sucks, our bosses are idiots, but that's OK because we know the next one will be better. Once we get the next one, we begin thinking about and planning for our retirement because that's when it is going to get really good! Have you noticed that this line of reasoning doesn't work?

Here's my advice. Yes, life is, and will be, hard. But hard is not bad. In fact, hard is how we make things happen. Physical strength, intellect, and character are built by hard. Flying airplanes, winning Oscars, and snowboarding double black diamond runs are all hard, yet these are awesome things. Every phase of life is full of hard things, so instead of running from them, embrace them and grow from them. Equate hard with strong, and strong with good, and you'll understand that loving and enjoying each phase of your life with its challenges and triumphs is really what living is all about!

EVERYONE GETS THE BAD—YOU HAVE TO MAKE GREAT HAPPEN.

Pain, loss, sorrow, loneliness, hardship, and death belong to everyone. They cannot be avoided, ignored, or escaped. In fact, the longer you live the more frequently you will experience bad things. As I mentioned, life is hard. OK, what about the good stuff? Doesn't it belong to everyone, too? Sorry, no, it doesn't. The prize patrol is not going to knock on your door and give you a million dollars; the prom queen is not coming over to ask you out. If you want something great, you are going to have to go out and get it. You must fight, strive, train, pay, and do it over and over again to get the great! But my friends, I swear to you by all that I am and all that I hold sacred, the great is worth it. Mount Everest, Broadway, the Amazon, Wall Street, pilots' wings, passionate love, adventure, and beauty are everywhere, waiting for the making! What are you waiting for? The bad stuff is going to happen no matter what. Let's go out and get some great. I have one other piece of good news: the great is much more memorable than the bad!

SPEND YOUR LIFE PURSUING WHAT YOU LOVE.

At the end of our lives, we may finally understand that there is absolutely no time better spent than the time we spend doing the things we love with the people we love. For me, success is a life spent pursuing our passions with people we love. Discovering ways to earn a living while loving what we are doing—that is success. Some are blessed at an early age with the knowledge of what they love most, and this is an incredible gift. The rest of us need to ask the question daily: what do I love the most and how can I make a living doing it? Get exposed to as many things as possible, travel as much as possible, continue your education, and stay true to your quest. Success is also found in the pursuit of a worthwhile goal, and there's nothing more worthwhile than discovering your true passion.

MASTER THE ART OF FAILING.

They say we learn more in our first four years in these bodies than during any other four year period, even college. Now, I've never been able to find out who "they" are, or why we should listen to "them," but I do quote "them" when it suits my purpose. I like thinking about those first four years because there is no other period in our lives where we fail as frequently. We can't do anything right. We can't talk, crawl, or walk. We keep making up words and sounds because we don't know the right ones. As we get mobile, we crash into everything, yet our bodies, minds, and nervous systems drink up this failure like a sponge. The magic of this period is that we have no fear of failure—it's pure trial and error. We fail and do, and fail and do, until we get it right, without judgment or condemnation. If we were born with our adult egos and a fear of failing, we would all still be rolling around on the floor cooing like babies!

Master the art of failing. Every time we fail, fall down, and lose, get beaten and bruised, we are given invaluable bits of information. Learn to digest it and act on it, so that the next time you try and fail, you will be a little better. Those of us with the courage to fail will one day find ourselves standing in the winner's circle!

LIFE IS SERIOUS, SO DON'T TAKE YOURSELF TOO SERIOUSLY!

By now, I really don't need to tell you how serious life is. Pick up any newspaper, turn on the news, and you can see that serious, important, and heartbreaking things are happening everywhere. You don't even need to pick up the paper—I know each of you is surrounded by drama, struggle, heartbreak, and pain. Fortunately, we have a weapon to bring to bear against all "the heartaches and thousand natural shocks that life is heir to" (thank you Mr. Shakespeare)—that weapon is a sense of humor. Learn to laugh much and laugh often. When you find others laughing at you, laugh with them. Laugh at your humanity, laugh at your weakness, laugh at your demons, and those demons will disappear.

I have shared with you my idea of a warrior: someone who can have his heart broken endlessly and never build a wall around it. Warriors achieve this by attacking heartache with humor, because only joy can heal a broken heart. Play your life like it is the most important game you will ever be involved in. Give it everything you have and everything you are, but never forget it is just a game! And games are meant to be fun!

Sharing my thoughts, musing, and adventures with you has been the work and joy of my lifetime. I hope that you have felt truly loved by me because you are. I hope that these words have brought you comfort, hope, and strength. And most importantly, I hope these words help you find your way home to love: love of self, love of this grand adventure, love of the people we share this adventure with, and love of the world we call home.

MAKE NO LITTLE PLANS; THEY HAVE NO MAGIC TO STIR MEN'S BLOOD
.... MAKE BIG PLANS ... AIM HIGH IN HOPE AND WORK.

DANIEL H. BURNHAM

Zenith Exercises

Zenith Exercise: Ending Into Your New Beginning.

Assume your focused meditative position. Sitting away from the back of your chair, check in with your body. Form ninety-degree angles in your major joints: ankles, knees , and hips. Begin your focused breathing in through your nose and out through your mouth. Inhale light, energy, and power; exhale negative energy, doubt, and stress. Continue this energetic breathing until you find yourself quiet and centered.

And now please join me for one last adventure together. We are going to mentally travel decades out into your future.

See yourself walking up the steps of a church. There is something odd and light about your movements. As you enter the hall, you see the chapel is overflowing with faces you know and love. You understand this is a funeral, and yet that word just doesn't feel quite right; there is far too much joy. You quickly and quietly find a seat just as the first speaker begins. An older person with the most beautiful voice begins telling the story of a brilliant life, full of love, service, connection, and adventure. You are touched by jealousy as you learn about this life lived so well. You reflect on all the silly things you have worried about and the people you have misjudged and hurt. You look down into your hands, and for the first time, you notice there is a bright white glow enveloping your body. The light grows brighter, and you can't seem to find your body's solid form. The brilliance continues to increase and begins fading out all of the beings surrounding you. Just as the audience begins laughing, crying, and clapping simultaneously at the story being told, you have life's greatest understanding! This end of life celebration is yours! You did it! You loved, played, and contributed. Not only did you live a joy-filled life, but also you brought joy to all those who had the privilege of knowing you!

Welcome Home!

Sermon on the Mount

You are the light of the world.
A city that is set on a hill cannot be hidden.
Nor do they light a lamp
and put it under a basket,
but on a lampstand,
and it gives light to all who are in the house.
Let your light so shine before men,
that they may see your good works
and glorify your Father in heaven.

Ask, and it will be given to you;
Seek, and you will find;
Knock, and it will be opened to you.
For everyone who asks receives;
and he who seeks finds;
and to him who knocks,
it will be opened.

MATTHEW 5:14-16, 7:7-8

PEAK PERFORMERS SKILLS SELF-ASSESSMENT

Grade yourself. On the exercise on the following page, give yourself a letter grade (A, B, C, D, F) for your current level of proficiency on all the Peak Performers Skills (PPS). This is a purely subjective exercise, but it is essential if we are going to create positive results in your life as quickly as possible. An A grade would mean that this PPS is second nature, and it is a skill you use consistently, naturally, and without thought. Scoring a B would mean that you use this skill well and frequently, but you must actively focus on it. Grades of Cs are pretty much a wash—you have used the skill at times, but it is just as frequently missing. Grades of Ds and Fs are pretty self-explanatory. A note on grading: this form of personal inventory is extremely valuable. It will give you a pretty good snapshot of your strengths and weaknesses.

	First Read	Training Order
+ Attitude	_____	_____
+ Balance	_____	_____
+ Confidence	_____	_____
+ Discipline	_____	_____
+ Enthusiasm	_____	_____
+ Focus	_____	_____
+ Goals	_____	_____
+ Heroism	_____	_____
+ Imagination	_____	_____
+ Joy	_____	_____
+ Knowledge	_____	_____
+ Love	_____	_____
+ Motivation	_____	_____
+ No-thing	_____	_____
+ Optimism	_____	_____
+ Perseverance	_____	_____
+ Quality	_____	_____
+ Responsibility	_____	_____
+ Service	_____	_____
+ Truth	_____	_____
+ Understanding	_____	_____
+ Vision	_____	_____
+ Wisdom	_____	_____
+ X-tra Mile	_____	_____
+ Yes	_____	_____
+ Zenith	_____	_____

NOW GO OUT INTO YOUR WORLD AND LIVE THAT LIFE!
WITH LOVE, GRATITUDE, AND PROFOUND HUMILITY, I AM NOW, AND HAVE
FOREVER BEEN, YOURS!

BILL POETT

NOTES

NOTES

NOTES

NOTES

NOTES

NOTES